VOYAGING PETS

Edited by
Shelley Wright and Jackie Parry

Published in Australia in 2019 by SisterShip Press Pty Ltd

Part of SisterShip Magazine, NSW, Australia
www.sistershippress.com

Copyright © SisterShip Press Pty Ltd 2019

All rights reserved. Without limiting the rights under copyright above, no part of this publication may be reproduced, stored in or introduced into a retrieval system, or transmitted in any form or by any means (electronic, mechanical, photocopying, recording, or otherwise), without prior written permission of both the copyright owner/the Publisher.

Typset and Cover Design by Shellack Designers
Printed and bound in Australia by SisterShip Press Pty Ltd

National Library of Australia data:

SisterShip Press Pty Ltd, 2019, Voyaging Pets

ISBN: 978-0-6484283-5-0

Also available as a hardcopy/paperback: 978-0-6484283-4-3
In collaboration with SisterShip Magazine

www.sistershippress.com
www.sistershipmagazine.com

*For everyone who has taken care of, respected,
and loved an animal of any shape or size.*

CONTENTS

Foreword 7
Introduction 9

PART ONE: Salty Sea-Dogs 11
  A Faceful of Fleas by Alison Alderton 12
  Captain Ivy by Lanise Edwards 15
  Scrappy Gets His Sea Legs by Robyn Hawkins 21
  The Bark by Jill Budd 27
  Things that go Bump in the Night by Sheenagh Neill 31
  Susie: A Dog on a Cat by Sarah Wilde 34
  It's a Dog's Life By Judith Maizey 40
  Losing Buster by Alison Alderton 45
  A Day in the Life of Miss Mel-Mel by Tanya Rabe 48
  Raffy Tails by Libby Taylor 55
  The Camping Chair by Alison Alderton 61
  Clueless: Tippy on a Monohull by Shelley Wright 62
  From the Farm to the Sea: Jemma's Big Adventure
  by Jill Hore 67
  Popcorn the Sailing Dog by Iona Reid (age 12) 73
  Sarsha's Story: Ye Old Sea Dog by Sandy Wise 76
  Lady Nugget takes on the World by Justine Porter 81
  The Reluctant Adventures of Hastings:
  A Boat Dog's Tale by Lucy Wilcox Claiborne 87
  The Big Decision by Carolyn Wasik 93

Please Remove DOG by Rosa Linda Román 99
Hudson "THE boat dog" by Kym Phillips 103
Ivy's Escape by Lanise Edwards... 107

PART TWO: Curious Cats 111
Listy the Barge Cat by Jane Chevoux... 112
The Night of the Big Tip: Tales from Cruising the ICW
(Intracoastal Waterway) by Dana Sims 117
Sailing with Pancakes by Lauren Demos....................................... 123
Flying Kittens by Jackie Parry... 127
How I Crossed the Atlantic Aboard a Sailing Ship
with my People by Daria Blackwell 130
All Paws on Deck: The True Story of One Cat's Transition
from Landlubber to Nauti-cat by Sandra Tretick 136
Walter Sam: Sailing to the Andaman Islands
by Jeanne Pickers... 142

PART THREE: Unusual and 'Not-quite' Pets 149
Roger Booby by Justine Porter... 150
Things Wot the Cat Dragged In by Jill Budd 154
A Ratty Tale by Cherylle Stone.. 158
Pet Kneaded on Board by Rachael Evans..................................... 160
Captain Patch, a Voyaging Guinea Pig by Megan Wright............ 163
The Life of Pi-Rat by Sydney Steenland (age 13).......................... 166

Acknowledgements 175
SisterShip Magazine.. 176

FOREWORD

Humans are naturally drawn to animals as companions; their innocence, unconditional love, and (usually) inability to be cruel simply for the sake of it draws us in. At sea, life can be tough, and the presence of an animal companion can bring joy at times when you truly need it, whether that be a troublesome wild bird making you laugh or a lifelong companion teaching you how to transition to life aboard with style and confidence.

As a veterinarian, a woman, and a sailor I have faced my fair share of challenges, none more so than the transition from landlubber to sailor. Reading of Hastings the dog's reluctance and eventual embracing of life at sea felt so familiar. The mistakes we all make, the constant learning, and finally the realisation that for all the problems that come with boats it only takes one amazing adventure to realise you can no longer imagine life any other way!

Although I spend my life rescuing animals, I like to think that they too have rescued me. I recollect one particularly nasty sail, with high seas and big winds. I was feeling down and disheartened with my abilities, when the sun suddenly peeked from behind the clouds and a pod of dolphins appeared. They were dancing on the bow, seemingly wanting to be watched and enjoyed. The frivolity and carefree nature of the dolphins instantly brought a smile to my face and reminded me why the hard times are worth it. This book will help you remember too, with beautiful stories of animals at sea, from all around the world.

To all the women who contributed, thank you for opening your hearts and sharing with us all what it truly means to enjoy life at sea with the presence of our animal friends.

Dr Sheridan Lathe, Founder of Vet Tails and Chuffed Adventures, Veterinarian, Ocean Nomad and Animal Lover, Proud Owner of SV *Chuffed*.

www.instagram.con/vet.tails_sailing.chuffed
www.facebook.com/vetotails
www.youtube.com/vettails
www.vettails.com

INTRODUCTION

Animals enrich our lives and pets can be important members of our families. People will go to extraordinary lengths to keep their families together, therefore taking a pet along voyaging is not that unusual. It is also not a recent concept. Throughout history courageous pets have sailed alongside equally brave seafarers.

Since people first began journeying on water animals have intentionally, or as stowaways, accompanied them. In early times, most animals on boats were kept for practical purposes (chickens and goats for food, cats for hunting), however these days our four-legged friends are more likely to be part of the family. They keep us company, ease stressful situations, and cause us worry, but in most cases, we wouldn't be without them.

While cats were perhaps more conventional on ships of old, dogs of all shapes and sizes (on an equally diverse range of vessels) can now be found in most anchorages. Voyaging critters are not limited to cats and dogs. Pocket pets such as rats and guinea pigs, although not common, are accompanying their doting owners aboard boats around the world.

The pets in this anthology travel across oceans or lakes, on day trips or week-long passages. What they all have in common are humans with an adventurous spirit who adore them. Sometimes, however, being onboard is not in a pet's best interest. Some of our writers share their heartbreaking decisions to do what is right as opposed to what they desire.

While it may be easier to travel with pets these days, it's not always smooth sailing with animals onboard. This selection of true stories highlights some of the highs and lows of life on the water with four-legged family. These are cruising companions who love their life onboard and add a new dimension of adventure for their devoted families.

These stories are from around the globe and across the age spectrum. Given the diversity of our writers (and their locations), we've left the women's own voices and kept the localised spelling to highlight the flavour of our international contributions.

We hope you enjoy this anthology and thank the many women who have contributed.

PART ONE: SALTY SEA-DOGS

A Faceful of Fleas
by Alison Alderton

In his youth Buster, our Beagle, excelled at catching rabbits. If quick, Roger or I could sometimes save the poor creature but, at other times, it would sadly result in a chase to retrieve a dead, dangling, bunny body from the vice-like grip of our hound.

Farndon Marina, our home on the River Trent, was bordered on one side by a series of small pools, the result of former gravel workings, and, in the small, grassy hillocks surrounding these, lived a large community of rabbits. Our group of dogs loved nothing better than snuffling about the rabbits' domain, hoovering up tasty, bite-size morsels of bunny pooh, popping their heads down burrows, digging furiously at the entrances or, once the bunny scent had entered their nostrils, generally running around as if possessed.

One afternoon, I was meandering back to the boat from this area when Buster made a sudden lurch on his lead, almost pulling me flat on my face. "For goodness sake, Buzz, do you have to do that?" Giving my arm a rub, I peered down at Buster who, slowly turning around to face me, revealed a smug look on his face and a tiny grey rabbit hanging out of his mouth. Oh no, I sighed. Acting fast, I took hold of Buster's muzzle and tried my best to prise my finger into the side of his mouth, but he was holding on fast. We struggled for a few moments before I stopped, recoiled, and watched in horror as thousands of tiny, dark-coloured specks began to crawl from the rabbit onto Buster's pure white muzzle and disappear beneath his fur. The rabbit was crawling with fleas and, as they sensed their host's life slipping away, they were making their escape — a mutinous crew abandoning a sinking ship.

I quickly came to my senses. One way or another, the rabbit had to be removed from Buster's jaws. I once again pushed my finger into the side of Buster's mouth and twisted it, prising open his jaw, shaking

Buster's head at the same time. The dead rabbit fell to the ground. "Good boy. Leave it."

Buzz looked at me as if I were mad. "Leave it, you've got to be joking?" he seemed to be saying. Buster made a desperate grab for the rabbit, but I was prepared and held firmly onto the shortened lead as he jerked and wriggled to reach it.

With the battle won, I gingerly picked up the still-warm body of the tiny rabbit and threw it into a dense blackberry bush. Thoughts of what to do with my flea-ridden hound then took over. Buster had flea treatment on, but I could not go back to the boat with him covered in them; they would infest the vessel. All I could think of doing was launching Buster into the waters of the marina. With his extending lead attached, I picked him up and begged his forgiveness. "I'm sorry, Buzzy boy, but this is for your own good," and, with that, slung him as far out as I could whilst keeping hold of the extending lead. There was an almighty splash as Buster hit the water and disappeared beneath it for a couple of seconds. On resurfacing, he threw me a glance of utter contempt. To say he was not impressed was an understatement.

"Come on, Buzz. That's it; swim to me," I encouraged, drawing in the extending lead as he began doggy paddling angrily towards the bank. Reaching dry land, he scrambled out and shook himself. Grumbling and complaining as only a Beagle knows how, he dropped down on one shoulder and rubbed his face into the ground. I felt dreadful; it was a cruel thing to do but it was a warm sunny day and appeared to have done the trick as most of the fleas had vanished. Just to be sure, back at *Lily's* mooring, Roger gave Buster a thorough "access all areas" bath with medicated shampoo, then hosed him down and dried him in warm, soft towels. Buster muttered and grumbled all the way through, telling his dad exactly what he thought about it!

Bio: Alison Alderton was born in Chichester, West Sussex and educated in the county: studying art, design and photography at the West Sussex College of Design in Worthing and later Creative Writing at NEC, Cambridge. For over 20 years she has contributed both words and pictures to leading inland waterways publications, belongs to several boating associations and is passionate about the world's inland waterways – she is rather fond of Beagles too!

Pet Bio: Buster the barge Beagle spent his whole life on and around waterways. During his 12 years he visited a total of 10 countries, seven of them by barge and lived full-time in five of them. Known as the Admiral, Buster travelled many thousands of miles and in doing so promoted our wonderful world of waterways to a wider audience.

Boating extensively throughout England, Ireland and northern Europe in Dutch barge Lily, Alison, along with her husband Roger and Buster have become well-known figures on the inland waterways circuit. Buster died in 2015, however, his life afloat is recorded in Alison's book 'Boating with Buster'. Now with their new Beagle, they are exploring Scandinavia and are currently based in Sweden.

Website http://www.alisonalderton.com/
Instagram https://www.instagram.com/lilyandthebargebeagles/
Facebook Page https://www.facebook.com/lilyandthebargebeagles/
Flickr https://www.flickr.com/photos/alisonalderton/

Captain Ivy by Lanise Edwards

Many said that we were absolutely crazy to contemplate cruising with an old black Labrador on a 40-foot monohull. There may have been some wisdom to these opinions. However, Ivy was coming along for the ride regardless. Hey, we are family, we stick together like dog fur to a salty deck. It's certainly had its up and downs though.

Years ago, as a puppy, Ivy's role model was our old Border Collie; Tilly. Tilly taught Ivy well and the main lessons were: Listen to commands but don't take them seriously, humans don't run the show – we do, and never miss an opportunity as you will be forgiven. These lessons appear to have stayed with Ivy for life, regardless of her formal education at doggy school. Ivy has provided us with copious moments of hilarious entertainment, along with a bit of added stress and marital tension! For the most part it has been worth it. Although I'm unsure about Ivy's opinion regarding her 'sea change', I think she enjoys large portions of life on the water with a few exceptions.

Sundowners, morning and afternoon tea, or just a cuppa with guests aboard *Easter Rose* are possibly not as common as they are on other cruising vessels. In fact, we seldom 'do' sundowners on other boats. This is largely because any guest must be a dog lover in order to cope with the experience. Of course, most cannot resist Ivy's charms, as she is very sociable and loves human company. I think she gets thoroughly bored with our chit chat and daily routine. This is where it gets tricky. Sundowners involve FOOD! You know; snacks arranged on decorative china plates, with exotic cheese and biscuits and spicy dips. Long stemmed wine glasses and cold chilled beer. I've seen blogs on how this can actually look. It definitely does not resemble this on *Easter Rose*!

Yes, we have the cheese and biscuits, dip, and whatever scrumptious nibbles our visitors bring aboard. However, it is never a sophisticated event on *Easter Rose*. I would describe it more as; 'let's test the guests.'

Here are some of our real-life examples: Recently we had friends aboard, they know Ivy well and she loves their company. I made some of those yummy little pastries with camembert cheese and sundried tomato, I was set to do this right. Our friends contributed lovely cheese, biscuits, and dip. Ivy likes to greet guests before they arrive by barking loudly and using her highly developed retriever scent to sniff the air for yummy morsels as the guests approach. Enthusiastically, Ivy salivates and greets guests at the only point they can climb onboard; the boarding ladder and step along side. At this point unsuspecting guests are at real risk of being knocked back into their dinghy or worse, into the water. Attempting to scramble onto *Easter Rose*, while wiping dog saliva from your face, is no simple feat. We are prepared and armed with strategies to help our guests, we attempt to subdue Ivy and try to encourage a gentler welcome for visitors.

Once aboard safely we all sit in the cockpit and around the back hatch. Plenty of room, however once we take our position it's hard to move around, *Easter Rose* is a monohull after all. On one occasion I emerged from the galley with my pastries and wine glasses, initially planning to use the aft hatch as a table top. On glancing up I noticed Ivy was sitting on the knee of our guest closest to the hatch, where they had placed cheese and dip. So, Tyler firmly pulled Ivy away from our visitor who was very polite, however clearly overwhelmed. They were covered in black dog fur and struggling to breathe under Ivy's 36 kg weight. Ivy just ain't small enough to be a lap dog!

Ivy knows how to sit and stay; however, she has always considered it offensive to have to follow these mere commands. I laughed and apologised to our guests, hoping they would forget the shambles already witnessed. I said, "Let's eat and cheers!" Obviously, Ivy thought this was a command she 'would follow' and like lightning, nosed her way onto the cheese plate, emerging with a large piece of double brie. She then jumped over our friend's lap with her heavy paws and claws, to access some enticing crunchy biscuits to accompany her exotic cheese. There was nothing hygienic or relaxing about this. Any person with a germ phobia would by now have dived overboard! My wine went flying and spilt behind the cockpit cushion, running down towards our guest. I raced below decks to grab a cloth and our visitors dived in to rescue the food, attempting to place it out of Ivy's reach. It was everyone for themselves and there was only one winner.

After sternly reprimanding Ivy, so as not to look like we had absolutely no control over her, we assessed which food was still edible. Ivy had obviously taste-tested a few morsels and several of my pastries. Dog slobber was evident and splattered all over some very nice cheese! Our lovely quests laughed and said, "It's ok, she is such a character". You know the way someone says your child is 'spirited' as they have a full-blown tantrum at the worst of times. Ivy did not appear fazed at the carnage and obviously was unaware that sundowners are not meant to look like this. By now she was licking our guests shorts as food had spilt on them, or was that wine, or dip? Our other guest was confronted with Ivy's bottom smack in their face as her happy-tail whipped their hair in all directions. I firmly told Ivy, "Go outside on deck," and growled at her. After a short period, our lovely visitors hear the ever so faint sound of an alarm on their vessel and politely state they must rush back to see what it is. Covered in dog saliva and spilt food they step into their dinghy. They smile and laugh and thank us for a lovely evening. Only the brave return to *Easter Rose* for Sundowners a second time.

Occasionally we are invited to sundowners, morning or afternoon tea with Ivy. Yes, I cringe and warn people about dog fur. Ivy has a beautiful thick black glossy coat that sheds constantly, and she leaves her mark wherever she goes. We are accustomed to this, however, it's a shock to pristine boat owners with no pets aboard. People say, "Oh it's ok she is a beautiful dog."

Ivy particularly likes catamarans and motorboats with large saloons and luxurious lounges. We discovered this after our first gathering on a beautiful catamaran.

Initially Ivy is the perfect guest, sitting contentedly with a small bowl of water. She adores the attention and pats and is prepared to behave like well-mannered royalty – for a time. This is short lived. When all the humans are relaxed and distracted, things change. If I'm alert and glance up, I will see Ivy sneaking in through the large accessible door, eyeing up a lovely leather lounge. Within a split-second Ivy will be rolling on her back on one of these lounges, rubbing her eyes and nose on the immaculate expensive cushions, snorting in delight and generally making herself right at home. If she can carefully plan her stealth move unnoticed, her next stop is the galley. Once her scent leads her to whatever nibbles are lurking on a benchtop Ivy is quick to act. With the slide of her tongue and the advantage of her height she is able to demolish most tasty treats rather fast. Now, if we catch Ivy in the act she freezes and looks as though she has no clue what we are on about. Even if still licking her nose where food may still be visible.

Visiting friends on monohulls like ours, is not as exciting for Ivy, as she cannot access the lounge or galley due to a companionway and ladder. You would think this is a positive for us however Ivy has other strategies. On one occasion we were invited for morning tea on a beautiful yacht. Our hosts had cakes and coffee on the table below decks and said Ivy was fine in the cockpit which was shaded and safe. I was relieved and thought this would be relaxing and easy. We began consuming cake and coffee while we chatted. Ivy watched from the cockpit. She was rewarded with a piece of cake herself, just so she did not feel left out. We continued chatting and I noticed our host became distracted and began to stare at the companionway steps and then glance back to our conversation. This happened a few times. I peered closer and Ivy had somehow produced enough saliva that it cascaded down the steps and it kept coming! If she could not be below decks, near the cake, she was sending her drool to reach it! I apologised and tried to mop up the steps. It's only natural for a dog, I know, however the amount of saliva that can be produced by one Labrador is quite phenomenal!

BBQs onshore are another favourite of Ivy's. She has been known to invite herself even if we are not attending! Not long after we moved aboard with Ivy, a group of boaties had a BBQ on the marina pontoon. They had set up a Weber BBQ, a table, and chairs in a half circle. The afternoon went by and I carried on with boat chores. After some time, I glanced out to see where Ivy was. She was not onboard. I looked up and down the marina finger and spotted her familiar black wagging tail. Ivy had invited herself to the BBQ and helped herself to steak and sausages. She then held full audience sitting in the middle of the people. Fortunately, they thought she was charming and gave her praise and pats. Little did they know she was eyeing off their plates for more food. As I ran down to collect our wayward pooch, she saw me and looked the other way as if she did not recognise who I was! Before I could attach the lead, she had a healthy lick of the Weber BBQ. People laughed, however they began to guard their food more carefully. Ivy's days of eating fatty food are now over as she has bouts of pancreatitis and her liver is aging. I'm not surprised given the amount of cheese and sausages she has stolen over the years! It's a low-fat diet for her these days.

I paint a dark picture of our beloved Ivy and have probably ruined our social life on the water forever with this story. However, for all her acts of defiance, her obsession with nibbles, along with her attraction to luxury catamaran and motorboat saloons, we love her. It's our fault that she thinks she is human as she lives with us 24/7 and is never left alone (that is another story for another day). Ivy has been part of our small family for a long time. She has incredible adaption skills and has managed to make her life on the water enjoyable, even in her old age. Intensely loyal (other than around food), Ivy has coped with some uncomfortable passages like a true sailor and exudes more love and forgiveness than we thought possible. Take us or leave us, we come as a package even at rare sundowners. 'Fur family' have always been a large part of our lives and with that comes some chaos and a good dose of dog fur. Fortunately, most friends we have met on boats adore our cheeky Ivy and think she is full of charm. Ivy certainly reciprocates this affection towards many cruisers who are missing their own pets. Her popularity in marinas and anchorages is obvious, until it's time to mingle, with the scent of food in the air!

Bio: I live full-time aboard SV *Easter Rose,* a 37-year-old monohull, with my husband Tyler, and our ageing dog Ivy. We've been heading north very slowly for three years with a few pauses in our journey.

Pet Bio: Ivy has adapted well after moving aboard having lived on land for 10 years. Now 14 years old, she still manages day to day boat life well. Ivy has always been a bright spark, a real character, and definitely not the most obedient Labrador in the world. However, this trait has likely assisted her to cope with our adventures at sea. Life is never dull with Ivy even in her old age. She is loyal, loving and has an eye for an adventure, wherever we are.

Ivy (Lanise Edwards)

Scrappy Gets His Sea Legs
by Robyn Hawkins

On the 18th October 2014, a litter of tiny puppies was born in a warm, cosy farmhouse nestled in the rolling Welsh countryside. We didn't know it then, but one of those puppies would become a treasured member of our family.

I drove home on a cold winter's evening from a hard day of teaching, walked in the front door, and was promptly told to close my eyes and hold out my hands. I did as I was told whilst wondering what on earth my partner, Dave, had been up to. I didn't have to wait long. A small, warm, squirming puppy was placed into my outstretched hands. My eyes flew open. Sitting in the palms of my hands was a tiny, chocolate-coloured puppy. My heart melted in an instant. Staring back at me with large brown eyes, wrinkled forehead, floppy ears, and light brown quizzical eyebrows was the cutest thing I've ever seen in my life. My very own puppy to love and care for. After much deliberation, we decided to call him Scrappy as he looked very much like a character from a well-known children's TV series (but smaller!).

Scrappy is a miniature Jack Russell. He has such a warm, loving yet playful personality, and captures the heart of anyone who looks his way. We love him probably more than we do each other (if that's possible!). When we decided to go travelling, he most certainly was coming along for the ride.

Dave and I are country bumpkins; I don't think we could have lived much further from the sea while growing up. Despite this, we decided to buy a boat, cast off our lines, and go travelling together.

Scrappy was almost as awkward as I was when we first moved aboard. Every step on deck was taken with great trepidation for fear of falling overboard into the murky brown waters of the Humber. Non-slip bath mats were laid down below deck as though royalty would be coming to stay. Nothing but the best for our little boy.

Day by day, we both grew braver and began to explore our new home with greater enthusiasm. Scrappy began leaping up from the cockpit and streaking down the decks to greet whoever was walking past our bow at the time, barking at the top of his voice. As a result, he quickly earned his title as 'Chief Security Officer'. Every movement on the boat was carefully monitored – he began to distinguish our footsteps from other people's and changed his greeting accordingly.

The day soon came for us to leave the dock for the first time with our precious cargo on board. It would be a new experience for Scrappy; I was keen for him to enjoy it. We took our time, only heeled over slightly, and made sure that he was always safe and happy. He began the journey down below, nestled in a pit of cushions and duvets. Once Dave and I were happy with how we were sailing, it was time to bring Scrappy into the cockpit – dressed in his small-but-perfectly-formed lifejacket, complete with robust carry handle – so he could feel the wind blowing on his face and rippling through his fur.

His initial sail was a great success, and, after more practice, it was time to make our first long crossing.

The weather wasn't as kind as we had hoped it would be. The hours rolled by as we were tossed and turned by the raging sea. I retreated below decks to lie down, leaving Dave in charge (alongside a friend who was accompanying us en route). I burrowed below the duvet and soon had a furry, warm body snuggling up beside me. We kept each other company during the long, wet, and windy passage, and we each had a calming effect on the other.

It was a baptism of fire for the three of us; we were glad to have had our more experienced friend on board as crew. After that journey, we began to choose weather windows for our passages more carefully. We haven't had to contend with anything as unpleasant since.

Scrappy has lived on board with us for the past sixteen months, and his confidence has grown in leaps and bounds. He has become a true salty sea dog.

One of the biggest challenges we faced in bringing Scrappy on board was the process of toilet training him. As a puppy, he was put outside every hour, on the hour, to ensure there were no accidents in the house. This worked well, and the larger he (and his bladder) grew, the longer we left between toilet breaks. We doled out praise and Scooby Snacks (treats!) until he cracked it, and – *voila!* – we had an incredibly well-toilet-trained dog. (Until somebody gives him tummy tickles, that is – it tends to make him pee all over their feet in excitement!) This made life very difficult when we moved on board, however. No matter how much encouragement or praise we gave him, Scrappy just would not pee (or poo) on the boat! We tried all sorts of tactics. We gave him a special spot to use, sprinkled grass on the deck, bought him a special mat (which we may or may not have peed on ourselves for encouragement...), but still no joy. If he was desperate and we gave him tummy tickles, then he'd go a little bit – but only by accident. There had to be another way.

When we stopped in Jersey over the winter, we were given a berth that was a 5-10 minute walk to a green area where he could go to the toilet. The pontoon was made of plastic and was full of holes that Scrappy kept catching his nails in. After weeks of uncomfortable journeys to the grass, he point-blank refused to walk on it. So, at least three times a day, we were CARRYING Scrappy up the pontoon so that he could relieve himself. Over winter. In all weather. Sun. Cloud. Rain. Horizontal Rain. Fifty-knot winds with freezing cold driving rain. Scrappy still had to go.

Something had to be done.

Fortunately, we found the best pet shop in the world. We stumbled upon 'Pets Paradise' on one of our wanders around the town and ended up chatting with a member of staff. We told him about our failed attempts at trying to toilet train Scrappy. He told us to wait; he had an idea. We mooched around the shop, wanting to buy everything (as usual). Ten minutes later, he reappeared with a big long piece of the artificial grass used to line the shelves in a greengrocer. It was exactly what I had been looking for since before we moved onto the boat. The best thing? He said it was ours – for free! I almost hugged him.

Toilet training, take two...

We tummy tickled. We praised. We bribed. We said "go toilet" far too many times. We cancelled all walks for a few days so that he couldn't cheat and go while we were out. We put him on the 'grass' first thing in the morning, when he is always desperate to go. We praised and bribed some more. And, by some sheer miracle, he peed. On the green mat. Hallelujah!

We kept it up all day for the next few days. We let him wander up there whenever he felt like it and, after a couple of days, he pooped on it! I practically danced on the boat in my pyjamas in full view of the entire marina.

It wasn't consistent at first, but, through countless Scooby Snack bribes and a massive amount of praise, we now have a BOAT toilet-trained dog! Woohooooo!

He's still not keen on going on passage, but he can, and he has done. We are no longer tied to 24-hour passages. Hell, we could go and cross an ocean with him now!

Re-toilet training a dog is hard work, but it was most definitely worth the effort. I no longer have to get dressed stupidly early and carry him down the pontoons in horrendous weather, and we can now go wherever we want! Yippee!

There have been many other highlights and milestones on our trip because of having Scrappy on board with us.

One day, when Scrappy and I were walking along the pontoon at the beginning of a long, energetic walk ashore, he spotted a duck. It was sitting minding its own business – just chilling out and having a breather on the edge of the pontoon. Scrappy decided that he would like to go and say hello, so off he shot towards the duck. What he forgot, though, was that he was attached to my hand by an extendable lead. It kept going and going until it locked off – just as Scrappy was attempting to round the corner to where the duck was sitting. He was catapulted in the direction of the duck, but the lead didn't quite go far enough for him to make it to the pontoon. There was a large splash as he made his unplanned and undignified entrance into the water. A rather miffed, bedraggled Scrappy was scooped up and put back on the dock while the duck swam away. It had lived to quack another day.

Another big problem was that Scrappy initially hated water with a passion. On rainy days, puddles were avoided as though they were smouldering pits of lava. Life on a boat has changed all that, though. Long daily walks along the seashore, playing fetch with balls that happened to land in rock pools, and treasured possessions (twigs and pinecones) being flung into the shallows have cured him of his fear of water. Now he will happily wade into water to retrieve items and swim. Watching his tail twitch from side to side like a rudder is great fun while we cheer him on from the sidelines.

When the weather is bad, we enjoy getting cosy and snug on the boat, but we always make sure Scrappy gets some form of stimulation to keep him occupied. One thing we really enjoy is creating a Scooby Snack trail for him to sniff out. This basically involves us putting Scrappy in the bedroom while we hide treats all over the boat for him to find. Once the Scrapster is released, his nose is glued to the ground; sniff mode is activated on high alert. He finds the treats one by one and devours them within seconds. We're always finding new places to hide treats and new games to play so he is kept happy on board.

Bringing a dog to live with you on board a boat is a major adjustment to their lives and yours. We thought long and hard about everything that needed to be considered – from food to vet appointments and vaccinations, and if he would be happy with his new life. It's a decision we didn't take lightly, but we are so glad we brought him along for the trip. He has opened far more doors than he has closed: he is a talking point everywhere we go, as everybody wants to make a fuss of him; he has become a happier, healthier dog because of it. I firmly believe that Scrappy is getting as much out of this trip as we are. He gets a new playground to explore every time we go somewhere new, he samples new foods, and he absolutely adores meeting new people and making friends wherever he goes.

Scrappy is part of our family, and he has made this trip so much better by coming along for the ride.

Bio: Robyn grew up in the land-locked county of Shropshire. She was introduced to boat trips and the sea during childhood family holidays but moving aboard *Baremka* (her 1974 Dufour 34) in 2017 was a whole new experience. Since moving onboard, Robyn has learned a whole host of new skills (including learning how to sail!) and has adapted to life on the water well. She now can't imagine living back on land!

Pet Bio: Scrappy is a four-year-old Miniature Jack Russell who moved aboard a 1974 Dufour 34 along with his parents (Robyn and Dave) in

2017 to go sailing around Europe. He is one of 'The Three Mutineers' and features regularly in videos published on his Mum's sailing channel on YouTube - 'Sailing Mutiny'. Scrappy loves walking on the beach and meeting new people, but isn't keen on having his bum sniffed.

Website: www.sailingmutiny.com
YouTube channel videos: https://www.youtube.com/SailingMutiny
Facebook Page: https://www.facebook.com/sailingmutiny
Instagram: https://www.instagram.com/sailingmutiny

Scrappy swimming (top) and with Robyn on the North Sea Canal, Amsterdam (bottom) (Robyn Hawkins).

The Bark by Jill Budd

Baxter was the first dog that came into my life as an eight-week-old puppy. All our previous dogs had been older and rescues; but the local dog sanctuary wouldn't let me adopt because I didn't have a garden so, against my principles, I went out and bought him. For the first four years of his life we pounded up and down the same stretch of beach together on our daily walks and then mated him, keeping one of his puppies, before deciding to retire, sell up, and move on to a boat and travel.

Our first boat was a narrowboat and we cruised the inland waterways of the UK for six glorious years – I say cruised but, for nearly all of that time, the three of us walked whilst my husband cruised the boat. We walked the towpaths, and I worked the locks and lifted bridges. On non-cruising days we did big circular walks exploring new villages, preferably encompassing a pub en route with a pint of real ale for me and a bag of pork scratchings for the boys.

Fast forward five years and we now live on a Dutch Barge travelling through mainland Europe. Baxter is nearly 16 now and I have become his carer. I can do nothing and go nowhere without considering his safety, comfort and well-being. His bladder and back legs are both weakening, his eyesight is failing, and his hearing has gone. It doesn't happen overnight – it's more insidious.

It starts when you're cruising and he's barking because he needs a pee and you have to find somewhere to pull over. Then it happens again; but you are too late, and he pees on the back deck. Then he barks because he needs a poo, and there is nowhere, absolutely nowhere, to pull over amongst the commercial shipping and, after a highly stressful 30 minutes, he eventually poos on the back deck – his look of shame and remorse breaks your heart, so you cuddle him and feed him biscuits, and re-think all future cruising plans to ensure that there is somewhere to stop every two hours maximum.

Then there are the mooring issues; will you be able to find somewhere to moor where the bank is at the right height for him to get off? We purchased an extra wide gangplank to increase his options but, as his back legs started to slide out sideways from under him, we had to abandon that one – even with its non-slip rubber mat covering. Then we used a footstool for him to jump onto; that worked for a while.

The first time I realised he was losing his sight was when he fell in the river, in winter, in the dark, whilst I was staying on my own on a friend's boat. It was pitch black and he mistook their dark blue canopy for the entrance; he hit the canvas and down he went into the fast running river between the boat and the bank. His lead stopped him from being swept away, and sheer adrenalin gave me the strength to haul him out.

Then there are the night shifts – we take it in turns to be 'on call' for The Bark, because The Bark comes before wees and poos. Unfortunately, now, The Bark also comes before, "I want to sleep where the cat is", "I'm hungry", "I'm lonely", "I just feel like making a noise", and "Why have you left the room?" Days out exploring together on our travels have become a thing of distant memories, one goes out whilst the other dog sits. Occasionally, if we can find a suitable mooring for him close to town, we might manage a lunch together within our 'two-hour' time slot; we can't take him with us, as he will only walk about 20 metres before planting all four feet and refusing to budge.

It's hard – the sleep deprivation is the worst; especially when I'm on my own (which I am quite often) for two weeks and am 'on call' around the clock. Here's a 'day in my life' when I'm on my own:

The Bark comes at 5.00 am (one of the better nights). Pull on shoes and coat, grab the torch (it's pitch black) and help his back end up the steps across the wheelhouse and out onto the back deck. After a wee he needs a poo, so he insists on getting off the boat. Help him off, line him up on the non-slip matting on the pontoon, stand on the mooring rope (so that he doesn't trip over it), and aim towards dry land. Reverse the process on returning, only this time, lifting his 16 kg up because he's too sleepy and wobbly to get himself back on.

Next time The Bark comes it's 7 am; repeat the extrication process. Head for shower (me - not him) and remove PJs; hear The Bark (surely he doesn't need another poo – perhaps he does); abandon shower and pull clothes on – nope, it was the, "Why have you left me?" Bark. Have a quick wash and clean my teeth. Make runny boiled egg with soldiers for breakfast and take the top off; here comes The Bark. By the time I get back the egg yolk has congealed.

Now he's asleep, so time to get started on painting the bedroom wall. One hour in and I'm head first under the top bunk, precariously balanced on one elbow with a can of paint when I hear The Bark. I ignore it. The Bark gets louder and more insistent until I can ignore it no longer. I unsnarl myself without throwing paint everywhere and find that the insistent bark was to tell me that he'd peed on the floor and that it was, 'all my fault', which it was because I ignored The Bark. Now it's time to put his dinner in to soak and walk the other dog for an hour. Get back and feed them both. Out for another wee (him – not me). Back under the bunk bed to finish painting the wall. At 6 pm I realise I still haven't eaten, so feed myself. Snatch an hour or two and try and do some editing before starting on the bedtime routine of persuading him to take his medication and his bedtime treats before taking both dogs out, individually, for last walks. Return to find the lights have gone out and so has the water pump and I've got to go down the engine 'ole and change a fuse. It doesn't fix the problem, so I give up until the morning. Go to bed.

Two hours later I'm woken by The Bark.

After a week or two of single handed 'on call', I could desperately do with a couple of dog free days; but I daren't, because those two days might be the only two days we have left together and I don't want to miss them and I must be with him at the end – it won't be long now before The Bark ceases and my heart will break.

Epilogue
Baxter was put to sleep on the 10th December, quietly and peacefully, at home on his own boat.

Bio: I was fortunate enough to take early retirement at the age of 54; selling my craft shops and moving onto a narrowboat to cruise the British inland waterways with my husband, two dogs, and two cats. After 6 years, we shipped the narrowboat across to mainland Europe and loved it so much that we stayed; selling the narrowboat and buying an elderly Dutch Barge. We still continue to cruise throughout Europe and you can follow our travels on my blog *contentedsouls.com*

Pet Bio: Baxter was a Tibetan Terrier. He would have been 16 on 3rd January 2019.

Baxter (Jill Budd)

Things that go Bump in the Night
by Sheenagh Neill

Let me introduce our beautiful, boisterous, bouncy dog, Rufus. He is a pure sable Kelpie, a new breed for us. If I was honest, I would say he is probably better suited to a farm, or younger, more active, people – but he chose us.

He is extremely loyal, and we love his company. Since he was a puppy, we have taken him out on our yacht. It was an abrupt introduction to the movements of the sea, the constraints of the boat, and boating life. After first being quite nervous, he now knows how to handle himself. He knows where our boat is berthed and happily runs and jumps aboard, waiting for us to depart.

When we aren't visiting National Parks, he always comes away with us. He is a great boat dog and loves seeing any marine life. He is fascinated by dolphins, penguins, and fish. His favourites are the seals, because they bark.

We were on a cruise with eight other yachts for a clean-up day on the shores of Great Bay, Bruny Island, Tasmania. We spent the morning collecting debris from the shores around the rocky bays that are only accessible by water. With the wind increasing and funneling up the D'Entrecasteaux Channel, we all met at Simpsons Point.

There we anchored and after a break we shared a lovely BBQ lunch on the shore. Several of the yachts decided to stay overnight a few miles further up the channel in the shelter of Barnes Bay at the anchorage of Rosebanks. After reaching the anchorage, some enjoyment, and sundowners, we all retreated to our boats for the night.

While I settled into our cabin, my partner took our dog for a long shore walk. Rufus has never-ending energy. He can easily go for a 10 km run and on his return bounce and spin in the air as if to say, "More please". After his walk Rufus was fed and we all retired for the night.

It was a relatively calm night with not much wind or noise, just the occasional lapping of waves on the hull, or chain movement. Noises at night on water seem to be more amplified. A vivid imagination can run riot with any efforts to sleep.

I became restless and my dreams were full of highs and lows, brightness and stars, like the beautiful Aurora Australis down here. My subconscious was alerting me to noise. Was that water splashing? Was that a bump? Was that the boat? "Relax go back to sleep, it's safe," I told myself. I'd been a sailor for long enough to know what can be ignored. I tried to relax and get back to a deep sleep.

At the same time, on a nearby boat, another crew member, as restless as me, was awoken by what she thought was a seal or dolphins swimming and fishing near her boat. She got up and looked out of her porthole, but it was so dark she could only make out something dark swimming by. Back to sleep she went.

Another skipper on the opposite side, heard similar splashing sounds but dozed back to sleep.

After falling asleep, it seemed only minutes had passed, and I was jolted awake in the early morning by the buzz of a text coming in. It was from the crew member who had thought she'd seen a seal in the middle of the night. The text read: "Is Rufus on board?"

"Of course he is!" I went to check, suspicious. Sure enough, there was no Rufus!

I texted back, "No, he's not on board."

She replied: "Look to the shore, he's sitting there near the waterline just staring out to your yacht."

Up into the cockpit I went in my PJs to see a sad little dog looking very ragged on the shoreline, sitting patiently facing out to us. My partner dressed and went and collected him. When he returned, Rufus went straight to his mat, tired, but very happy to be on the boat.

Later that morning at a shared morning tea we all discussed the night, the cruise, and how Rufus ended up on shore. Theories about Rufus's antics from the night before flew around the cabin. In conversation several sailors mentioned their restless night full of dreams of splashing seals and other dreaming stories. We laughed as we looked at Rufus and came to the same conclusion. We suspect

Rufus went to shore perhaps to relieve himself but then when he swam back in the pitch dark, he couldn't work out which boat was ours or how to get back onto the swim platform.

So, after swimming around several of the nearby boats, past portholes and cabins, entering people's dreams, Rufus sensibly swam back to shore some 100 metres away.

The exact circumstances of that night will never be known. Clearly, he had a night he hasn't forgotten! Rufus has never ventured off again. Just in case, he's always tethered at night these days.

Bio: Sheenagh Neill is the immediate past Vice Commodore of The Cruising Yacht Club of Tasmania (CYCT). She is also a member of the Kingborough Boating Club and Bellerive Yacht Club. She is an active member and admin of the online group Women Who Sail Australia and runs several online groups and pages to support sailing or clubs in Tasmania. As a strong advocate of equality and women-can-do-anything, Sheenagh is a co-skipper of her yacht *Tahiti*, a Jeanneau Sun Odyssey 42i. She loves all things boats and updates her knowledge regularly through forums, meetings, and training.

Rufus (Sheenagh Neill)

Susie: A Dog on a Cat
by Sarah Wilde

We were Susie's second family. When she came to us, she was a Golden Retriever with a weight problem, claws like a bear and a soft and trusting nature. She loved children and being fussed, she was less keen on walks.

As time went on, she became fitter and enjoyed long walks with the growing children, especially in the mud around the Somerset levels where she would come back two-tone with a deep brown lower half and pale yellow above the tide line. She was also more than happy with her life jacket on out in the canoes or on our trailer sailor, sitting with her tongue hanging out watching the world go by.

When we started planning our big adventure, travelling on a sailboat, there was never any question that she should come with us. We did however have to think about all the complications that having her with us would bring. A dog passport, how do we find dog food? What if she's scared? What if she's ill? We worked our way through all these things, putting together a plan. A long discussion with the vet, a dog first aid kit, insurance; there were lots of things to sort. Possibly one of the most practical things we purchased was a tag with our mobile phone number, boat name, and registration number for her collar.

We were ready and moved on board our 42-foot catamaran. Susie decided she wanted her bed under the chart table and made herself comfortable. She took to boat life straight away. Sleeping in the sun on the deck and joining in with boat school by sitting up on the cockpit bench or lying under the table. She had people with her nearly all the time and new exciting walks, not to mention the strong fishy smells of the harbour sides which seemed to be particularly enticing.

Teaching her to use the deck was our first big challenge. We tried all sorts to encourage her to see the deck as a garden and somewhere she could 'go' so that we would be OK on the move and when anchored.

There was Astroturf on the deck that had been in our garden for a couple of weeks so that it would smell right – she wouldn't use it. There were puppy training pads, she wouldn't use them. We tried keeping her on the boat hoping that desperation would encourage her; she just kept her legs crossed for longer and longer. Finally, the penny dropped, and she spent it on the deck. We were all very relieved. She would wander around the deck and settle down in the sunniest spot. The skipper put lifelines around the edges – partly for her, partly for the children.

We travelled along the south coast of Britain. When underway she was not allowed out on the deck on her own. If it was calm enough just a lifejacket was enough but in any other conditions, she was kept on a lead just to make sure we didn't end up with a dog overboard. She enjoyed meeting new people, sniffing new places and having us around all the time. She was happy to be left at times if we were going to a museum or somewhere else she couldn't join us, something I had been concerned about before we left. Retrievers are a breed that likes their sleep and she was as safe inside the boat as she would be in a house.

Always happiest when with her children, she loved curling up with the boys listening to bedtime stories. In fleecy pyjamas, with clean teeth, the deckhands would stroke her and fondle her soft ears whilst they listened intently to the adventures of the Swallows and Amazons. With curtains drawn and hatches clamped firmly down the boat would seem to glow with its lights and heaters on, cozy and homely, the world shrinking in that moment, filled with the story and the warmth of being together.

As Christmas got closer, the weather got colder. As we wore more jumpers and tried to keep the boat warm, we gave her more blankets to lie on. Then there was the evening that, feeling the cold, she slowly moved closer and closer to the heater until finally the smell of burnt fur filled the cabin. Fortunately, we realised what she had done, and everyone rushed to move her and turn the heater off before she knew what had happened. Apart from a singed patch on her coat she managed to escape without any harm.

Getting the final vet checks done before leaving England, we found several mistakes on the original paperwork that could have caused us problems further on down the line and a second microchip making her older than we had realised. Finding a vet with experience in pet passports is really worthwhile. Finally, passport in paw, she was ready to travel.

We crossed the channel to France first. In Cherbourg she got a bit excited about going for a walk and tried getting off herself. A catamaran with a 90-degree swing around the sugar scoop to get off is not the place for a dog to try this and with a splash she fell into the water, swimming around in circles until the skipper hauled her out unceremoniously.

She was a people dog, sitting under the table, curled up at our feet or just being where her people were. Her walnut brown eyes meant that she was very good at pleading for scraps; she loved French baguettes as they are so flaky that she would get lots of crumbs. A typical retriever, she looked like she had a permanent grin on her face, always laughing, often dribbling. There was a sticker we found in France which said *'Chien Feroche'* – ferocious dog, definitely not our Susie who a burglar would have to wake up to get a reaction from, but it went on the door of the cockpit because we thought it was funny. A couple of times people asked if it was safe to come aboard, pointing at the sign. They were always surprised to meet Susie and find her rolling over for a tickle.

She would always greet customs inspections as a chance to get fussed over. Only once was her passport given more than a cursory glance and that was because the customs wanted to know what her name was.

At Lezerdrieux things became very dramatic with her overexcitement about going ashore and she fell off the front. She had her lead caught on the front cleat and was hanging by her collar off the front of the boat over a fast-flowing river. At a loss to what to do for the best and knowing that something had to be done quickly, she was physically hauled up hand over hand and pulled back onto the deck. How she was not injured by this is anyone's guess. She was extremely lucky.

Further down the coast of France we went, then across Biscay to Spain. For two days across the notorious bay she kept watch on her little family. Curling up around the base of the helm's seat, at each watch change she would make sure everyone was settled, snuffling at whoever was off watch until they fell into a deep sleep in the cockpit, before returning to her spot under the helm. We discovered that she could hear dolphin pods long before we could see the tell-tale splashes. Head on one side she would look down at the sole of the cockpit then sure enough within a short while there they would be leaping and playing around the boat.

She loved being in the dinghy, wearing her bright lifejacket and hanging her tongue out. Hauling her into it and back on the boat was entertaining at times, shoving and pushing her up onto the sugar scoop or throwing her over a shoulder to tackle a ladder.

Walking to places we wouldn't have found without her was an unexpected bonus of her company. Evenings wandering around a place, trips out beyond the bounds of a marina, or taking a different road because you were just walking rather than setting out to see something specific. Off the boat she would find grass to roll on, turning herself upside down, paws waggling, wriggling her hips side to side.

In Gijon on a busy pavement near the city centre she decided she didn't want to walk any further and lay down refusing to be persuaded to stand up and acting like a sea anchor on the end of the lead every time anyone tried coaxing her to move. The crowds had to part to walk around her laying on the pavement until eventually the skipper had to pick her up and carry her. Another winter came around. On stormy days in harbour she would curl up around the base of the helm as if we were at sea.

Staying in a casa in northern Spain was an eventful week for her. There were lots of big windows, something she was less familiar with since moving on the boat. She tried walking straight through one, bent her nose backwards and left a big snotty nose print on the glass. A few evenings later she found an open gate and had a really nice walk down the lane sniffing as much as she wanted without being told to hurry up. Realising she was missing we all set off in different directions calling and whistling. She was found wandering casually back up the lane towards the casa, who knows what she'd been up to in between, we were just all so pleased to see her.

Moving through the Basque country and back up the coast of France we changed from jumpers to shorts and t-shirts. In the heat of the summer we took to keeping her cool with a small fan, some days walking only first thing in the morning or late in the evening once things had cooled down. We took a folding water bowl everywhere with us. In Spain and some parts of France there are many public water fountains where fresh cool water can be found.

As our adventure continued it was increasingly obvious that her journey was coming to an end. She was slowing down and struggling with her hips. Where the tidal range makes ramps particularly steep at low tide she had to be carried. Walks became slower and slower until if we wanted to go for a long walk, we had to leave her behind.

Reaching Brittany, we were close to the end of our time travelling, soon we would be returning to England. We were staying ashore in a rented gite in France with family when it was clear that our time together was ending and that she would not be returning with us. The days had dwindled, and her body could take no more. After 14 years, there were no more years left. She died peacefully in a warm room with all of us around her, stroking her and telling her how loved she was. Long lashes closing one last time over those deep brown pools. The owners of the gite offered to place her alongside their own companions surrounded by flowers and apple trees. The sky was clear and the birds singing as we carried her to her final comfortable spot where she could sleep forever peacefully in the sun. She now lies in a beautiful French orchard and will always remain in our hearts. Our first sea dog, Susie.

Bio: Sarah spends as much time as possible with her family on adventures of all sizes. She lives on a river in Devon and has a blog about living on a boat, writing and taking photos.

https://sarahontarquilla.blogspot.com/

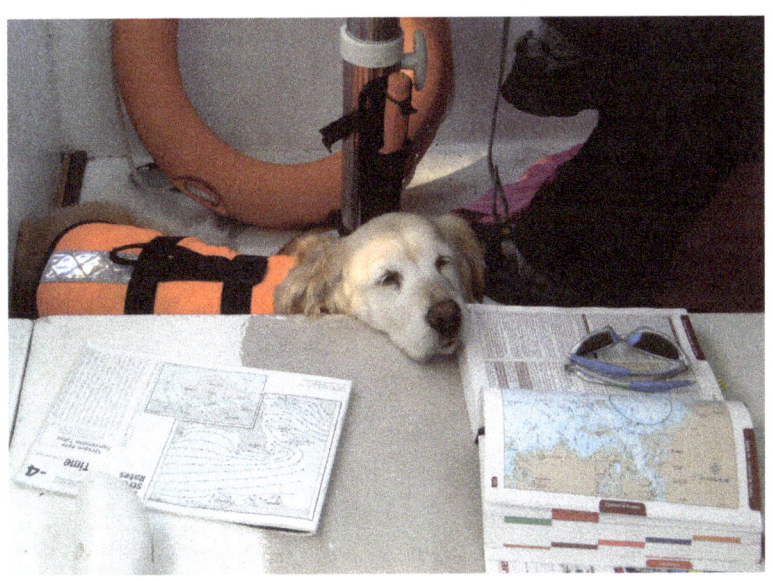

Susie (Sarah Wilde)

It's a Dog's Life
By Judith Maizey

Faster than a speeding bullet. Is it a bird? Is it a plane? Is it Superman?

No. It's Super Suki – the fastest dog on any east coast beach in Australia.

Let me formally introduce myself.

My name is Suki. You can call me Super Suki if you like, I don't mind. Just don't call me late for dinner because I do like my food, particularly treats. I am small and extremely loveable – a black and white miniature Fox Terrier. Female, seven years old or thereabouts and for most of the year I now live on Mum and Dad's boat. My mum tells me I was the runt of the litter. I'm told that explains my 'attitude', but I prefer to think of myself as sassy.

Anyway, enough of me (for the moment), my first home was a big house on acreage. But when I was about three, this boat came into our lives. A biggish boat of 16 m without sails, with a dark blue hull and two big motors. She's called *Ionian Sea* and is a Seahorse brand if anyone cares to know.

Like my mum, I'd never spent much time aboard a boat before the good ship, *Ionian Sea*, was purchased, but once I got the lay of the land (excuse the pun) I liked it. I don't actually get seasick as such, not like Mum, but I'm not a big fan of those long-drawn-out trips. By long, I mean 10 to 12 hours. They're so mind-numbingly boring for me I pretty much just loll around in my nautical trimmed, blue and white striped doggy bed and snooze.

It's not until we get to our destination that I come alive and go into action. You should see me jump into our bright blue tender when Dad gets it off the top of the boat and brings it around to the duckboard. I literally fly.

But it's when I am on the beach that I really come into my element. I reckon Olympic sprinter Usain Bolt would find me a worthy competitor racing up and down the sand. In fact, he might even have to eat my dust. As I said in my introduction, they don't call me Super Suki for nothing. I am like greased lightning.

In shallow water chasing bait fish, I am a tad slower and am yet to even catch a fish, but I'm improving and persistent. So focused am I on catching those slippery little critters, I just can't hear my name when Mum calls for me to get back in the tender. That water splashing around my ears is deafening. It's only when I stop to catch my breath, look around and see Mum storming towards me with a cranky look on her face that I realise I must move quick if I am to redeem myself.

Once in the tender, my preferred position is standing on the bow like one of those majestic figureheads at the front of the old-fashioned tall ships. It's only when Dad kicks the motor up to top speed and waves start breaking across the front that I make my way back to sit on Mum's lap like a Princess. From there, I hope she protects me from getting drenched and becoming a projectile if Dad hits something in the water – like a sandbank while going flat out.

Back aboard the big boat, I generally receive a treat for being good. Even when I don't come back straight away from catching fish, I still have a treat. I just put on 'my poor, poor me' face and look remorseful. My cuteness proves irresistible and I am rewarded.

Just recently, I've started sitting on the front of Mum's kayak to go ashore which is okay except when she miscalculates paddling and I get an accidental bonk on the head. I am, however, getting better at ducking so that's happening less frequently now. Thank heavens.

So, for others thinking of taking fur babies like me aboard their dream boat on their dream journey, let me share with you some pearls of wisdom I've garnered along the way.

First, your fur baby needs to be adaptable. I have a half-sister – a mini foxie, Maltese cross called Sugar (although she's not as sweet as me) – who just does not get boating. She cannot jump from the dock onto the duckboard without falling in. She cannot effortlessly or intuitively jump from the duckboard into the tender, and vice versa, because she is understandably terrified of falling in. She does not like standing at the front of the tender like I do instead she sits quivering like a bowl of jello at Mum's feet. She does not like the sensation of the waves or the noise of the engines. As far as I am concerned, she's a lost cause and if you ask me, she's never ever going to get cruising, so she stays at home with Mum's real baby, her land-based daughter, and only occasionally comes aboard for visits – short visits.

My second piece of advice is that your boat needs to be set up, so we fur babies don't fall down stairs, through hatches or overboard which really is the worst-case scenario for us more than you. *Ionian Sea* is not too badly set up for fur babies. If the transom door out to the duckboard is shut, I can't fall off the back and when we are travelling from one destination to the next, I'm not allowed out the front on the bow unless it's dead calm.

I am allowed to check out the dolphins and whales if they come alongside while underway, but generally when the engines are running I'm tucked up in my doggy bed on the seat behind the helm in the pilothouse.

And, lastly, but probably most importantly, you need to commit as fur baby parents if you are taking us with you. That means you need to take us ashore rain, hail or shine for a run and toilet stops whenever and wherever possible and you can't get upset if we have little accidents aboard.

I have a puppy mat set up in a kitty litter tray on the back deck which I use when I can't get ashore. It's not my preferred option, but it does the job. I have been known to pee on Mum's rug in the galley. I don't know why. I just do. It just seems the right spot at the time, but I do get into a wee bit of trouble because I am meant to use the puppy pad. I've also been caught short once or twice and pooped on the front deck, near the bow. Again, Mum wasn't impressed but she sort of understood.

So, while my peers and I can be vexing at times on a boat, we are a lot of fun and give unconditional love. In my case, I am the entertainer, Mum and Dad's little buddy and, most importantly, the circuit breaker.

Some of my more entertaining performances include cutting loose and running wild, going every which way up and down the stairs between the saloon and the pilothouse. It's exhausting, but it's in the job description. On the beach, my Superman impersonations where I run like the wind with my ears back and a silly look on my face also gets a laugh.

In my buddy capacity, I snuggle up to Dad while watching television until he or I fall asleep – usually it's me first unless that wildlife expert, David Attenborough, is on. I love watching some of those animals he films because they are seriously odd. Certainly, they make some of my antics look normal.

But it's when things go wrong, or the weather is challenging, and things get a tad tense between my two humans that I come into my own as the peacemaker, the circuit breaker, the conduit to peace and harmony. The dog whisperer.

For that trait alone, I know Mum is forever grateful and I will calm those darn waters every day of the week if it scores me an extra Schmacko... and, of course, her love.

So, you see, having a pet with you on your sea voyages has a lot going for it. It's not for everyone, but from a dog's point of view, I thoroughly recommend it.

Casting off for now.

Super Suki.

Bio: Judith Maizey – Suki's mum. In the prime of her life. Loves close family and friends, sundowners, writing and the beach. Hates running fast, particularly when it means chasing Suki

Pet Bio: Suki – mini foxie. In the prime of her life. Has disposition of a cat – haughty and self-possessed. Loves treats, the beach and being the centre of attention when it suits her. Runs fast and does not respond to her name when chasing fish.

Suki (above) with Judith (below) (Judith Maizey)

Losing Buster
by Alison Alderton

He had travelled many hundreds of nautical miles with me. Basked in fragrant summer days on calm waters, huddled close to me on cold, winter, ice-breaking explorations, and stood firm at the helm through raging storms but, now, he was gone.

Like a golden, autumnal leaf caught on a brisk breeze, he was wickedly snatched away. There was no warning. I was not prepared and, no one had forewarned of the heart-wrenching loss I would feel for months, years, afterwards.

Losing a 12-year-old dog, whom, since the age of 10 weeks, had become my constant companion was hard. Life-shattering. As he had grown up, matured, and eased into old age beside me, we had mellowed into life together, we knew how each other ticked, good and bad points, likes and dislikes. And, likened to an old married couple, becoming almost unable to function without one another. We were one – joined at the hip, as they say!

I immediately missed the gentle patter of his paws on the steel deck, the grumbling sounds he had made when he rubbed, shook and shimmed his back along the superstructure, the sound of his snoring when asleep in the wheelhouse, and most of all, the warmth and comfort of his body close to mine at night.

Death is one of those taboo subjects which nobody really wants to talk about or face. I had, in a previous life, been a funeral arranger, but that did not help the overwhelming feeling of guilt I had at my dog's passing. It was not death itself that was the problem. You see, I let him down. I let down my best friend of 12 years and 10 days on the day he died and that has been hard to forgive.

I had to leave my dog, my boy, by himself. For me, leaving his body with the vet, was the hardest part of his death. It was not because I did not trust my vet, it was because my dog and I had never been apart.

I felt I should place him in the ground, instead he was taken away from me. To lose anyone or any creature, miles from your homeland is difficult. In the past all my pets were buried in the grounds of my family's home, over one thousand miles away from where my boat now was. Because of this I was faced with cremation and what to do with the ashes afterwards.

I did not want them to sit on a shelf or in the boat but neither did I want to scatter them and never have a place to go to remember him. Eventually, I returned to my homeland by car, it involved a ferry ride, something which my dog would have enjoyed. That made me smile to myself.

His ashes were interred at my family home which stands less than a mile from the sea. Resting in a place he loved, I finally allowed myself to feel I had not betrayed him and began to let go.

No one likes to think or talk about the death of a beloved pet in any detail. Being on a boat, however, it may be advantageous. Having a plan, no matter how basic or brief, may help you face the uncertainty of what death brings. Like any good sailor who has an alternative port in case of foul weather, be prepared to take time out. Allow yourself to mourn. And, like all storms, eventually it will begin to pass. The rage will calm, and a glimmer of bright light will appear amidst the chaos left behind and, with that, comes hope.

For me, hope came in the form of a new ship's dog. It was not an easy decision to make: guilt gnawed away at me and I fought desperately hard to keep the new puppy at arm's length, feeling that, whenever I held him close, I was betraying the memory of the past. It was a fight I was never destined to win. The overwhelming feeling of warmth, love, and release of hurt when I hugged him to my chest could not be ignored, and to make him into a real ship's dog all my love and devotion would be required.

Buster (Alison Alderton)

A Day in the Life of Miss Mel-Mel
by Tanya Rabe

Pitter-patter, pitter-patter, pitter-patter.

One eye squints open. It's still dark.

Pitter-patter, pitter-patter, pitter-patter.

She will go back to bed any moment. I snuggle deeper into my soft, cool pillow hoping to catch up with my dream again.

Pitter-patter, pitter-patter, pitter-patter.

What if she needs to go to the toilet?

Pitter-patter, pitter-patter, pitter-patter.

"Ok! Ok! I'm up Mel."

Even fast now; pitter-patter, pitter-patter, pitter-patter, pitter-patter, pitter-patter, pitter-patter.

I stumble from our comfortable, cosy bed in the aft cabin into the main saloon, eyes barely open, trying my hardest not to step on top of the cocker spaniel dancing about my feet. The pitter-patter of her doggy toenails frantically connecting with the teak and holly floorboards. She is way happier than I am, that I am up.

It's dark in the cabin. I can see the half-moon beaming through the larger hatch as I lean in to take a closer look at the hands on the captain's clock. Four-twenty-five am.

"Mel! Really?"

At the sound of her name she becomes excited again; pitter-patter, pitter-patter, pitter-patter.

Mel's day has begun, and it seems, so has mine.

4:28 am

I've suited Mel up in her pink harness, so I can take her up on deck to go to the toilet. She's a funny little dog. A complete princess most of the time, very Meghan Markle; the people love her.

Her harness is on because when something catches Mel's attention, she suddenly becomes completely deaf, superbly ignorant, snubbing all commands. There's a good chance she will jump over the doggy-safety netting surrounding our decks and launch herself off the bow like a Red Bull adrenaline junkie. A huge problem for us (and her) because Mel can't swim.

Even though my peaceful sleep and romantic dream has been disrupted by Princess Mel's desire to start her day, I am feeling very thankful to be up on deck at this time of morning. The world sleeps, and we are surrounded by a stillness, a quietness that only occurs at this hour. I can see the reflection of the clouds mirrored perfectly in the water; as above, so below.

4:33 am
Back in the cabin and Mel is communicating very clearly to me that it is now time for her breakfast. I have been awake for less than ten minutes and I have a little dog launching herself up and off the sofa repetitively, bounding into and out of the galley, making little piggy snorting sounds and it is only a matter of time before the drool begins to flow. It's rare that Miss Mel will tuck into a normal dog's breakfast of some kibble type biscuits. That's only good enough for her when bacon or sausages are layered on top.

You will begin to see a distinct pattern developing as this story unfolds. We are not her owners, but her servants.

4:37 am
Her older brother Maxy, also a Cocker Spaniel, is wakened by the aroma of fresh chicken breast cooking. Together they stand peering at me from the entrance of the galley both with threads of drool pooling by my feet. Are they waiting patiently? Not one little bit. There is whinging, howling, the odd nip between one another and I am still wondering how my dream may have ended.

4:45 am
Both dogs are back in their beds sound asleep. Like I said, we are mere servants.

7:00 am
Just as I begin to prepare breakfast for Anthony and myself the spaniels are up again. They both come bounding along side by side, bouncing off one another ready to start the next part of their day. I'm sure the

reason they are up is because they think the servants are preparing a second breakfast for them, instead I'll put our breakfast on hold and we will go for a dinghy ride to the beach.

7:10 am
I believe Maxy and Mel to be direct descendants from Ivan Pavlov's dogs. They are a prime example of classical conditioning because as soon as I head toward the doggy locker, these two have started jumping, spinning, barking, and howling knowing that it is time for a D-I-N-G-H-Y ride to the beach. We never say the 'D' word aloud and in full until we are positioned at the D-I-N-G-H-Y.

7:15 am
With one spaniel on my lap and the other at my feet, we are headed to the beach. Long cocker ears are flapping in the breeze, mouths open, tongues dangling, both dogs wearing what we call their 'Dinghy Face'. Life's good in the world of Maxy and Mel.

7:20 am
As we near the beach Mel ambitiously tries to wriggle her robust, nuggetty little body free of the strong hold I have around her. Since moving aboard, I have become immune to doggy claws digging into my flesh from excitement. Maxy is the gentle dog, waiting patiently for us to lift him from the dinghy to the beach. Mel on the other hand is wrestling to get out of the tender on her own; legs, ears, snorts, slobber, claws. I have one arm secured around her body and the other with a white-knuckle grip on her leash.

7:20 + 10 seconds am
The four of us are on the beach!

7:20 + 12 seconds am
It is a stunning morning; the sky is a vibrant baby blue today, there's barely a cloud in sight. The slightest breeze kisses the back of our necks as we run along the shore together.

Maxy is completely trustworthy. He ventures only as far as we do, staying by our sides, constantly looking up at us to hear the words, "Good boy, Maxy" to which he responds with a cheery waggle of his stumpy cocker tail. There is nothing more important to Maxy than Anthony and me. Our Mel-Mel, now she is a whole other story.

7:21 am
One of the luxuries of sailing life is that from time to time you find yourself on your own deserted island with white sandy beaches and clear blue water. There was not another boat in sight or any trace of the humankind, just a pod of dolphins beyond our boat, a curious turtle checking out our hull and a couple of shy dugongs. Paradise.

7:25 am
Even though the shoreline permitted dogs off-leash I had always kept excitable Miss Mel-Mel on her lead. On this particular morning Anthony turns to me and calmly says, "Let's let Mel have a little run off the lead. She can't go anywhere." It was true, she couldn't get off the island, but something within me, call it women's intuition if you like, could foresee somewhat of a situation arising.

7:26 am
After a bit of toing and froing I relented, letting go of my fearful doggy mother thoughts and said to Anthony, "OK, but you had better be prepared to run." With that he unclipped Mel's lead, and within a split second, she bolted.

7:27 am
One minute is a very long time when you are watching your beloved little dog running away from you, especially when you see her take a turn into the water to chase a lone seagull who flirted with her unashamedly. It was dead on low tide as we watched her bounding further and further out from our island getting closer and closer to a neighbouring island. I looked at Anthony and without a word he, Maxy, and I started sprinting toward Mel who was mindlessly mesmerised by this seagull.

7:28 am
For one moment Mel turned around mid-bound to glance at Anthony who was trying to coax her back, but that moment was very brief, and she turned her head and kept going toward the other island. At this point the fearful doggy mother worry was overriding all logical thinking and my mind was flooded with 'What If's'. What if the water suddenly got deeper and there was a strong current? What if she stood on a stingray or a stonefish? What if she made it to the other island and we couldn't find her in the trees? What if that island went under water at high tide? Panic had arrived.

7:29 am
To our surprise she finally turned around but instead of coming back to us, she changed her course and headed to the back of our island which was not the same beautiful white sand as the front beach but mud! Here was our cute little golden cocker spaniel, the dog that butter wouldn't melt in her mouth, the Princess, having the time of her life. In tow was Anthony, slowed down by knee deep mud as he sucked one leg out of the sludge and sank deeper down with the other leg. I didn't know whether to laugh or cry.

Time Unknown
I lost sight of them both as they turned another bend. Maxy loyally by my side we waited. Eventually Anthony appeared with Mel by the scruff of the neck. He was wearing mud socks up to his knees and had splatterings of mud over his body and face. Mel was barely recognisable, completely covered in mud except her bright eyes sparkling and her mouth agape, tongue hanging out longer than I had ever seen it before.
I couldn't help myself, looking at Anthony I said, "I told you so."

Later That Day
Mel had a couple of baths. Anthony had a few hours' sleep to recover. Maxy got lots of treats and I had wine for lunch.
All's well that ends well. This is one story of hundreds of memories that we share with Maxy and Mel. I have simply adored having them with us on our sailing adventures.

Bio: Tanya Rabe (Dogs Who Sail). Hello, my name is Tanya. I'm Maxy and Mel's mum and am absolutely thrilled to be combining my two passions; dogs and sailing. Dogs Who Sail was created to celebrate our sailing dogs. It is my quest to provide fellow sailors with a big picture of what it really means to sail with a dog. We offer support and solutions to our Dogs Who Sail community with a hope to see dogs and owners share a memorable journey of life upon the water.
There are actually two creators of Dogs Who Sail, two amazing creatures who have changed my life in a thousand ways. They are not your typical bloggers but nonetheless will open up your mind to the possibilities of sharing your sailing adventures with your furry four-legged friends.

Pet Bios: Meet Maxy and Mel.

Maxy is a black Cocker Spaniel, bred from Grand Champions. I've had him since he was a puppy and he has been my loyal protector for 14 years.

Miss Mel-Mel is the gold Cocker Spaniel, our Golden Girl. It is with great sadness that I share with you that she was called to cross The Rainbow Bridge only a few months ago. She leaves me with a thousand stories and happy memories.

www.dogswhosail.com
https://www.facebook.com/groups/dogswhosail

Beautiful Miss Mel (Tanya Rabe)

Maxy and Mel (above), Mel and Tanya (below) (Tanya Rabe)

Raffy Tails
by Libby Taylor

I have undoubtedly earned my stripes as an old salty sea dog. My name is Raffy and at the age of 13 dog years (or in my 80s in human years) I can honestly say my life has been blessed. The most loved, pampered, and above all 'adventured' dog.

My family Libby and Bob Taylor own a Hunter 41 cruising yacht, *Synergy* and chose me specifically due to my Labradoodle characteristics. They wanted an intelligent, small 'big dog' that doesn't drop bundles of hair and is not smelly, and especially one that would embrace the high seas and challenges of living on a boat for an extended period. Now here's the catch. They adopted me from the breeder in the Hunter Valley, Tamaruke, as a stud dog. You heard right, it was intended that I would produce prodigies – more "oodles" to bring joy, love and devotion to lucky owners.

The slight hitch in this plan came when for work reasons they moved to the Sunshine Coast in Queensland and of course made the trek north with the boat and me. This meant that I was on occasion flown down to fulfil my obligations with willing little Labradoodle girls and earned me my very own frequent flyer points. The downside of course was the dreaded crate, which I was jammed into for hours on end and thrown into the cargo hold of a huge, noisy, flying machine. The above-mentioned reward for the ordeal in part compensating for this inconvenience and just added to my yearning for adventure.

My life of spirited enterprises started at the age of eight weeks when I was a small jet-black ball of fluff oozing with cuteness. I was introduced to my new family who promptly whisked me into their car and home to a house in Cammeray, with teenage boys, and of course their boat, which they used every weekend.

I'll never forget that first encounter with the boat – a floating, strange smelling, treeless, grassless, bobbing thing. Not to mention my paws had no traction on the slippery deck and where was I to pee? It was terrifying, especially when I was rolling around in the cockpit (as you do) and happened to accidentally slide off the back, plopping into the dark, salty, and freezing water. Instincts locked in and I immediately started paddling frantically towards the shore. No mean feat I can tell you with my hysterical parents having jumped into the water to save me. It's strange how humans have to be taught to swim and me only weeks out of the womb, could extend my little paws and stroke like a master marathon swimmer.

My life of loving water and frolicking in the ocean had started. Soon I was surfing the waves and consumed with the obsessive necessity and joy to chase balls. My love affair with tennis balls has never faltered and I am a genius at sniffing one out where ever I might find my self. Being a connoisseur as I am of the yellow delights makes me very discerning and if they are not Wilsons or Head tennis balls, I can't help but rip them to shreds. I know, I know! Bad boy! This is indeed a real personal failing as all my toys are still mostly intact 13 years later.

Without a doubt one of the biggest challenges of this boat life is the need to pee and on occasions of course poo. Being a boy requires the subtle art of lifting one's hind leg almost vertical and can only be instigated when my highly-tuned sniffer detects the right smell. Traversing the sloping deck, without falling overboard on rolling seas to the pointy end of the boat is a major feat of endurance and stamina. To make this feat easier, my parents installed a piece of fake grass tied to the side so it can be washed. And how clever were they! They got me to pee on it at the house before bringing the now enticing said mat to the boat. They also kindly put some netting along the safety rails, so they wouldn't have to jump overboard again in case I slipped. Not that they could have found me if we were underway as I am so black and would be impossible to see in a pitching ocean. They also bought me a lifejacket, complete with reflectors so when the sea got seriously rough, I wouldn't drown if something really drastic happened. The handle on the back also means I can be lifted like a 10-kilogram handbag and passed into a dingy – convenient but a tad disconcerting.

The move to Queensland of course meant playing on the beach every day, surfing, and meeting lots of lovely humans and their fur babies. It was doggy heaven. I have fond memories of our regular visits to the boat when it was at Tin Can Bay marina and made wonderful friends with a cat called Indy. She was so much fun. She would chase me and hide behind the power poles and then pounce on me. When it was my turn to chase her, I would jump on her boat, find her rather strangely feathered toys and often left-over cat food – much more delectable I have to say than dog food. Cats certainly are a strange species too – for one, they simply can't run properly, scampering sort of sideways. They have a peculiar sense of humour and are definitely very sneaky. Indy would find it most amusing to pay pre-dawn visits to our boat, wander around, and spy on us soundly sleeping, me cosily tucked up on my parent's bed. I really do feel sorry for those crate-trained hounds that are locked in a kind of sleeping box at night, unable to guard against any invasion from the likes of a duplicitous feline.

An excruciatingly embarrassing experience also happened to me at Tin Can Bay marina when I was walking along with Dad and he stopped to talk to someone we knew. I have no idea what came over me, but the chap said, "Someone has just pissed on my foot." I still don't know what came over me that day, I guess it was his alluring smelling footwear that got me going. To make matters worse this story is often told at Sundowners on a sandy beach to a cast of many.

A highlight of my life has been the opportunity to meet and spend time with my daughter Suki, a cute, petite blond. As a wee pup she was flown to Townsville to her new owners, our very good friends. We formed a welcoming party at the marina as she arrived and talk about the fuss the humans made with everyone adoringly ooooing and ahhhhing. I couldn't believe my eyes – she had inherited my love of squeaky balls! Did we have fun! We spent a few weeks together romping on the beach at Horseshoe Bay on Magnetic Island, and other anchorages, and I was able to show the ropes with sand digging and swimming.

She also mastered the peeing mat very quickly. It probably helped that I generously offered to pee on the mat to get her started. I am telling you I have a bottomless tank, especially when I unload on irresistible tree trunks, as those that know me would attest to.

I have to admit... I have another somewhat overwhelming obsession. I need to supervise the catching of fish. When we trawl for fish behind the boat the sound of the reel going off sends me into a complete frenzy of excitement. That huge flapping fish being hauled in puts me on high alert with my tail furiously wagging. I honestly can't stand the thought of eating raw fish or even worse killing one. But seriously they need to be controlled and made to calm down. Snapping at them and putting my paws on them clearly helps, although my parents don't seem to appreciate my input, and often tie me up to the steering console. Tethered to the console doesn't deter me from my mission though. I still contribute with some rather loud barking and yapping. I just can't help myself either when we are on a beach or anywhere humans are fishing – just the thought of that slippery cold sea creature brings out my alpha hunting instincts.

My interest in sea creatures also extends to my finely tuned ability to talk to dolphins, whales, and batfish. The first encounter with batfish was in Blue Pearl Bay in the Whitsundays where a number of very friendly, enormous, roundish fish appeared at the back of the boat. I jumped down close to the water and stared at them, my sniffer twitching, and at the same time making a sound resembling a guttural cross between a growl and yap. It's kind of like a human hummmmmm or grrrrrrr. I can hummmmmm or grrrrrr indefinitely when occasion calls. Anyway, it certainly gets their attention and they look up at me awe.

Dolphins and whales on the other hand are much smarter and rather larger. They too talk to me, dolphins kind of squeak and hang around surfing the bow of the boat whilst whales shoot water fountains and make a singing sound which is very noticeable when down below. I have a fond memory of a time when we were anchored in Hervey Bay in September, which is the whaling breeding time with many baby whales around. It was my mother's birthday and Dad organised for a mother whale and her baby to swim close to the boat and roll on its side and wave to us. Needless to say, I thanked them profusely with lots of tail wagging and grrrrrrring.

Now for a not so pleasant memory. One day I nearly died. Marinas can be very dangerous places fraught with slipping hazards and peeing challenges, given it is totally frowned up to lift one's leg on a power pole. Our boat was in our marina berth in Mooloolaba marina where a number of boaties reside, especially during the nasty cyclone season. It's a very friendly place, close to the beach with lots of parks and great playing areas for fur babies. I was having a little nap on the seat in the cockpit with one eye keeping watch for anyone passing by. Along came the most stunning and gorgeous smelling Labradoodle girl – she was chocolate coloured, about my size, with beautiful soft ears and a spectacular tail that was wagging with a rhythmic beat. Well I jumped to attention, standing erect and alert to show off my handsome and virile physique. I just couldn't help myself as I launched my younger self off the back off the boat in an attempt to land on the marina finger. Alas, unbeknown to me, the wind was pushing the boat away from the footway and I misjudged the gap, plummeting into the murky water below. My mother was down below, and I had nowhere to go, as it was impossible to paddle to safety.

Now unlike humans, dogs can't scream or even bark when they are submerged in cold water. I thought I was about to have my last adventure as I slowly sank below the sea. It felt like eons as my adventurous life flashed through my brain. Then suddenly a warm hand grabbed me by the scruff of my neck and collar, hoisting me airborne and depositing my rather soggy and bedraggled body onto the marina. My pride was shattered, and my confidence took a serious dive but I was alive. This taught me a lesson in marina logistics, and, to this day I have never dared to jump ashore unless my parents coax me across the abyss.

I have many more tales to tell, as my life has been full of intrepid experiences and I am a testament to the saying "an old dog can learn new tricks."

Bio: Libby and her husband have owned their Hunter 41 cruising yacht, *Synergy*, since 2000 and have spent extensive time sailing the east coast, living on their boat for four years between 2012 to 2015.

Pet Bio: Raffy was born on 19th February 2006 and is a black Labradoodle.

Raffy (Libby Taylor)

The Camping Chair
by Alison Alderton

"Be careful, the canvas isn't very strong." I warned as Roger lowered himself into Buster's camping chair. Buster was doing the rounds, sampling all the outdoor seating to see which suited best. Despite religiously practicing the routine he would always return to his faithful old chair even though the canvas was becoming saggy and threadbare.

"Doesn't look as if I've got much choice," Roger grinned at Buster who had, for the time being, pinched the newest chair and was busy perfecting his snoring, his muzzle nestled into the arm rest.

One of the sausages sizzling on the barbeque burst with a loud pop, sending meaty juices dripping onto the hot white coals and aroma into the evening sky. Buster's nose sprung into life, twitched, and fidgeted before he opened his eyes and fixed his gaze on the succulent meal cooking. Slowly he adjusted his vision, focused on Roger and frowned.

"Now you're in trouble." I giggled watching Buster's frown deepen until a baggy rift of fur hung above his eyes. With a disapproving groan, Buster leapt out of the chair he had looked so settled in, raced across the grass and sprung onto Roger's lap, sending us into hysterics. A few seconds passed before our laughter was interrupted by the sound of tearing cloth. There was a look of horror on Roger's face as our eyes met and the canvas seat gave way. With Buster still on his lap, he plummeted to the ground, bottom first through the metal framework of the chair. I could hardly contain myself watching my husband and hound rolling about on the dew-damp grass entangled in the metal framework and ripped yarns. Following a hard day's boating their cabaret act was perfect entertainment.

Clueless: Tippy on a Monohull
by Shelley Wright

I grew up with dogs, but when it came to boats, we'd only ever had cats aboard – until Tippy.

Tippy came into our lives as *Adam* about a year after we'd bought our first 'big boat', an Endurance 35. Tippy clearly did not see himself as an *Adam*, however, as he very rarely responded. Local dog obedience club days left me feeling somewhat silly bellowing "ADAM" as he stared aimlessly at his feet. We decided a name change was in order and, given the white tip on his bushy tail, he became Tip. (Ironically Tip's registered show name was 'Jayess Wats-a-name')

Tip was bred as a show dog. He led a sheltered life in a neat suburban yard before finding his way to our chaotic menagerie in the Australian Alps during the first year of his life. He eased happily into country living, gradually losing his fear of screeching cockatoos but developing a hatred for magpies (something we never fathomed) – the mere sight of these handsome piebald birds threw him into a frenzy of barking. As Tip became part of the family, we discovered he really was the most uncoordinated and least agile dog we'd ever met. He had no concept of climbing – either up or through – and had to be taught how to scale the four short steps into and out of the house. We had no concern that he might stray as he was flummoxed by a single strand of wire that most dogs would have ducked beneath or stepped over in the blink of an eye. Ironically, he was a Shetland Sheepdog, a breed known for agility skills.

Despite the presence of a creek that snaked through our high-country property and the antics of our water-mad border collie, Molly, Tippy showed no interest in water at all. This was probably a good thing given his long coat, short legs, and the extreme sub-alpine weather. As our boat was moored some 600 kilometres away, we chose to leave the dogs with family whenever we made the journey to the water. A move to the Hunter Valley when Tip was two years old meant we were suddenly within easy reach of the boat and day sails were now possible.

One day, for some long-forgotten reason, we decided to take Tippy out for a sail – just as a trial (sadly Molly was no longer with us). Complete with bulky bright yellow life jacket, Tip looked the part and happily waited to be lifted into the car. Have I mentioned his lack of agility?

At the boat ramp near our mooring, while we readied the dinghy, the kids attempted to lure him into the water with treats. The aim was to at least get his fluffy feet wet. This much was achieved, much to the amusement of passers-by and other boat ramp users watching as a flood of praise was heaped upon this slightly pathetic looking dog standing in five centimetres of water!

In addition to his lack of agility, Tip was large for his breed, weighing 16 kilos. Imagine struggling with a sack of potatoes into the dinghy. Once in the dinghy he would lean all his weight against whoever was sitting next to him. On reaching the 'big boat' transom ladder (there was no way of getting Tip aboard this way) one of us would climb aboard and undo the gate in the lifelines while the others placed the dinghy strategically below. Carefully balanced, one person lifted from below and the one on deck grabbed and then pushed Tip along the deck at the same time rapidly clipping the lifelines closed again before he could roll overboard.

When the time came to reverse the process and head to shore, he would stand helplessly in his doggy life jacket, frozen to the deck, waiting to be man-handled unceremoniously back into his floating chariot. Safely in the dinghy he would look immensely pleased with himself. It didn't end here though, upon reaching the shore where most dogs would bound from a dinghy to dry land, this helpless pooch would wait expectantly to be once again lifted out. The only way he would jump was if we tipped the dinghy on such a tilt that he could step gingerly ashore. With feet back on dry land he would stand with an extremely satisfied grin, proudly wagging his tail while we told him what a *CLEVER* dog he was.

Once ashore there would be 'pee-mail' left by other salty sea-dogs to check before leaving his own messages for future four-legged wayfarers. Unless desperate to 'go', shore leave was often an extended affair as Tip became distracted by smells, found revolting things to eat, and completely forgot why he was there and what he should have been doing. Following him around, plastic poop bag in hand, as the shadows lengthened and our minds on sundowners, could be a frustrating experience. Oblivious to the impatiently waiting humans behind him Tip's shore leave was often punctuated by periods of standing staring vacantly into space rather than getting on with the job at hand.

Mission finally accomplished, back on board (having been through the 'get Tip onboard without anyone straining a back muscle or going overboard' routine again) Tip would park himself on the cockpit seat in front of the companionway hatch – meaning those wishing to go below or come back up had to scramble carefully over him risking life and limb.

Endurance 35s have a high pilot house and a large flat foredeck – lots of room for spreading out and moving around. The deck between the coach house and gunwales is easily traversed by people but is more challenging for a fluffy barrel on four legs, worse still if the aforementioned is clumsy as well. There was little chance Tip would knowingly climb through the lifelines (remember that strand of wire?) but every chance he would try to turn and fall between them, therefore it was with trepidation that we watched him traverse from the cockpit to the foredeck. A jib sheet lying a few inches above the deck was enough to stop him in his tracks. Although eventually he learned to pirouette (more like a rhino than a ballerina) if he had a change of heart half way along, or came across a jib sheet, most of the time returning to the cockpit involved walking backwards ever so carefully.

Having Tip aboard while underway added a whole new level of worry. While sailing on a reach he would decide he *could* actually climb the cockpit combing after all, and that now would be a great time to leave the safety of the cockpit for a stroll along the LOW side of the boat. The crew would leap to action, coaxing him back to the cockpit where he would sit wistfully gazing in the direction of the foredeck. When he did finally settle, it was more often than not on top of the main sheet – creating more problems if a sudden loosening of the sheet was in order.

When we were anchored, Tip liked to take himself onto the foredeck to sleep or watch passing boats. He was safe there, or so we thought.

One particular evening we found him perched perilously on the very end of the bowsprit, the sea breeze blowing his handsome sable locks as he posed like the stars from the Titanic movie. He was, however, quite stuck and at risk of tumbling overboard. Panic reigned, he was retrieved and from then on, the staysail bag barricaded the pulpit rendering the bowsprit inaccessible (again - remember that single strand of wire?).

Life was never dull when Tip was aboard!

Earlier this year, aged 12, Tippy left us, too soon. While days aboard the boat are now less stressful, hairy, smelly, or difficult, the tippy-tap of his feet on the deck above and soulful eyes looking down the companionway steps are missed. Clueless as a boat dog he might have been, but he was a much-loved member of the crew.

Bio: Dr Shelley Wright is a scientist and co-editor of SisterShip magazine. She sails an Endurance 35 *Orac* with her husband Steve on the east coast of Australia.

www.sistershipmagazine.com

Pet Bio: Tip was a much-loved sable and white Shetland Sheepdog, an old soul in a clumsy fluffy body.

Tippy

Tippy (Shelley Wright)

From the Farm to the Sea: Jemma's Big Adventure
by Jill Hore

How will a 10-year-old, but still energetic, farm dog adapt to life at sea? I've had a bit of experience, but Jemma had only been on board our previous catamaran years ago, while in the marina or motoring in the calm waters of the Gold Coast waterways.

Now we had bought a monohull – 37-foot Jeanneau Sun Odyssey – and needed to drive 2,000 km north to take possession and sail her back to Brisbane, slowly. We retired and intended to become semi-permanent liveaboards. Would she be happy? Would *I* be happy? There was only one way to find out.

She knew something was up, and when the ute was packed, there was no way she was going to be left behind. Never a relaxed traveller, she stood, with her tail jammed between her legs, all day from 4 am until 7 pm. The next day she was so exhausted that she actually lay down for part of the time while we were cruising on the highway, jumping up when we came to a town. On the third day, we arrived at the marina to be met by friends who helped lug all the gear onto the boat, giving Jemma a confused but exciting introduction to her new home.

I was nervous about her jumping onto and off the boat, insisting on lifting her. She hated it and showed how happy she was when I finally let her jump up and down by herself, on my command.

There were several modifications/upgrades to be done to the boat before we would be ready to set sail. One of the first was to install some safety netting, as much for my sake as for Jemma's. Perhaps not aesthetically pleasing, but great for peace of mind and useful for drying fenders, shoes etc without them falling overboard.

Jemma loved the marina life. She came with me every time I made use of the facilities and on extra walks, meeting several of the locals doing the same thing. Life was a social whirl! She even got to play with her beloved ball every morning at the boat ramp car park.

I carefully invested time giving the command to "Have a wee" or "Have a poop" so she would understand my command. I had some false grass matting that I had rubbed on her fresh wee. I had collected both hers and other dogs' poops, to get the scent onto it. I placed it in the back part of the cockpit where the previous owner's dogs had done their business – within reach of the salt water wash down hose. No amount of encouragement would induce her to use it, on or off the boat, wherever I put it. Well, why should she use that, when I would soon be taking her for a walk anyway? I even tried showing what I wanted by using it myself. The disgusted look she gave me was priceless! Not too discouraged, though, I was confident that she would soon use it if we didn't go ashore for several days.

A couple of months later, and we were ready to leave. A friend came with us on a short shake down trip, to help keep me calm, refresh my memory of crew tasks, and become familiar with this boat's systems. I was seasick, but Jemma seemed to take it in her stride. We were away for three days (two nights). She held on the whole time. As soon as we got back and took her to the grass at the marina, she let it all go. Wees first, then lots and lots of poops. Oh well. Perhaps next time?

Then we were ready to leave. The northerlies had arrived, and the summer cyclone season was fast approaching. Time to get out of the marina. We had not sailed this far north with our previous boats, so the area was new to us. What beautiful scenery – lush, tropical vegetation, islands, mountains, and the gorgeous blue sea.

We are no heroes, and we don't have deadlines to meet, so we try not to get caught out by rough weather, but occasionally it happens. Sometimes we just couldn't dinghy ashore on a daily basis. When this happened, Jemma would hold on and hold on until she couldn't settle, she just prowled around, then got the shakes, then eventually would relieve herself where I had been trying to get her to go all along. Yay! Good girl, well done! What a lovely girl! Surely now she will be happy to go there when she's ready. Nope.

I've tried kitty litter. She avoids it like the plague. I've tried a plastic "puppy trainer" with fake grass over a grate with a collection try beneath. No way. She became so distressed when I kept trying to get her to do a wee or a poop, she would hang her head and push it between my legs, or under my knee if I was sitting down. I gave up. We know she can hold on for 36-48 hours. We make every effort to go ashore every day. If we can't, and she can't wait any longer, she will eventually go where she's been told to. That's just the way it is.

Apart from that, she has adapted pretty well to the new lifestyle. She doesn't like rough seas, but then neither do I.

She just loves being with us. If neither of us are in the cockpit, she'll sleep on her bed in the companionway. As soon as one of us comes up, she's up on the seat right next to us, often lying on a leg or foot, but always close.

She doesn't seem to want a lot of exercise. She has a few major excitements in the day. She gets to sleep on her bed on the little patch of floor in the aft cabin. In the morning, when she hears me roll over and get up, she slinks up to the V-berth for a quick pat, then back to the companionway stairs to impatiently wait for me to get dressed and help her up the steep stairs. We do a few laps around the deck, play catch with her soft rope toy, then hide and seek with it somewhere forward of the cockpit. She has become quite good at sniffing it out. After breakfast, if possible, we'll go ashore briefly, then back to the boat to get underway, or just relax with me reading in the cockpit.

If we're sailing and the conditions are good, she'll snooze. If the conditions are rough, she'll stand with her tail jammed between her legs so hard it pokes out near her tummy. All the while she gazes at me, willing me to pat her. How can I resist?

Do dogs get seasick? Yes. Occasionally. Once she has emptied her stomach (why is it always yellow?), then she settles down and is fine.

Each of us has our daily tasks. Jemma's is to keep the swallows away. She takes this *very seriously*. The faintest 'cheep' has her ears up and every part of her *alert*. She completely ignores any other birds. It's only swallows that are the enemy. Although if she sees a cormorant land on our solar panels, she watches it intently until one of us notices and convinces it to depart.

She makes sure we don't forget when it's dinner time, becoming my best friend ever about half an hour beforehand. When it's dark and she's ready to join us downstairs, she stands at the companionway looking meaningfully at the stairs until I am ready and say OK. Then she hops over the wall and launches. All going well, I'll catch her and take her weight just before she lands. It doesn't always go smoothly, and a yelp lets me know I've stuffed up. She gets lots of sympathy and apologies and goes to bed. All is forgiven.

Marinas are great fun. She won't walk without a stick in her mouth, drawing lots of smiles and comments. Nearly everyone loves to see her, so she's learned to greet everyone with a tail wag and gentle nose on the leg. I know people only recognise me if I've got Jemma with me – which is most of the time. We even have friends who only ring up to see how she is! Our welfare comes a poor second.

I think on balance she has enjoyed the sea change. I've certainly been proud of her – of her ability to adapt to new experiences, and always of her obedience and affection. I do think, though, that she's looking forward to that race out to the front gate at the farm, when we get back.

Bio: Jill worked in IT then HR before retiring to join her husband, cruising the Queensland coast of Australia - heading north as the temperatures drop, then south to sit out the cyclone season on their boat in Moreton Bay, or back on the property in northern NSW. Whilst her husband has always had boats, she only saw the light relatively recently when they purchased their first boat in 2010.

Pet Bio: Jemma, too, is a late comer to sailing. She is the product of a passionate love affair between Jill's husband's SNAG (Sensitive New Age Guy) Border Collie "Harry" and a friend's delightful stray Kelpie inappropriately named "Puppy". Prior to her Big Adventure, she had spent her whole life on the farm, with just the occasional trip to the first boat while it was safely docked at the marina.

Voyaging Pets

Jemma

Jemma (Jill Hore)

Popcorn the Sailing Dog
by Iona Reid (age 12)

From the very first time we saw each other, Popcorn and I both knew we were going to make the perfect team. We first met at the house where she was born, where I was introduced to Popcorn and her two brothers. The boys ran straight past me, whilst Popcorn curled up on my lap. My family all wanted a different dog, but I insisted that we take Popcorn home, and I eventually got my way.

For about a month, Popcorn and I spent as much time together as we could. When she was ready to face the water with me by her side, we went down to the sailing club. Popcorn was so excited that as soon as we went on the dock she jumped straight into the water with no warning. We hauled her out, and she tried to jump in again, but luckily, we caught her this time. The first thing we bought after that was a lifejacket to keep her safe, and to give us something to grab onto when she tried to jump in!

Since then, Popcorn has joined me on the water in my Topper as long as it is not too windy. Over the past two years she has become very good crew. Sometimes she helps balance the boat (well she tries to anyway) and has even managed to do a dry capsize. She keeps me company when the wind drops, and we are not moving much, but has been known to fall asleep at the bow! Occasionally, Popcorn does perform one of her very annoying habits. As Popcorn loves to watch all the sailors go by, it means she runs around wildly getting in my way! Overall, Popcorn has become such good crew that she even earned her own trophy. For the very first time the sailing club presented 'The best canine crew' award, and she was very happy with it.

As well as enjoying sailing, Popcorn also loves going into the powerboat, because her ears flap around more at that speed. She is always welcomed by the other sailing club members and is popular with the other juniors who love her cuddly and friendly habits... especially when she joins me in the Halloween dressing up!

Popcorn has helped me raise around £500 each for two charities as part of our joint Charity Sailing Challenge (CSC). Whilst I focussed on raising money for WaterAid, Popcorn has been raising money for Guide Dogs (because she is not big enough to be one herself). The Guide Dog organisation were so pleased to have this support that they sent representatives to watch us sail at the club, including a real live Guide Dog called Minnie. Our CSC activities have earned us two awards which we are really proud of. One from my school (George Spencer Academy, Chilwell, Nottingham), and a trophy from my Scouts' troop (2nd Chilwell).

Popcorn is a great crew and, even though she can be mischievous at times, she can also be very cute. I hope we have lots, and lots, and lots more adventures together and she can learn not to get in my way.

Bio: My name is Iona Reid, I am 12 years old, nearly 13. I love to sail with my beloved dog Popcorn (who also loves sailing). When I am not sailing, I love climbing (even though it's really tiring). I sail at Attenborough Sailing club, and I live in Chilwell.

Popcorn and Iona (Iona Reid)

Sarsha's Story: Ye Old Sea Dog
by Sandy Wise

Well, I have to start this story by saying our Sarsha is not just a pet she is part of our family, and her Border Collie/Staffie heritage made for a very intelligent little being. She wears a short black and white coat including a black eye patch and presents herself as quite a pretty young lady. Sarsha grew up on our boat as it was being built. When the boat was launched, there was no gnashing of teeth as to whether Sarsha would be coming or not. She was our surrogate daughter. Our own children were well grown by now. From the time she was a puppy Sarsha loved being anywhere we were. She slept beside our bed for the ten years we were in the house and came with us to the shops and to barbecues with our dog-friendly friends and relatives. Our 'hooman' children would refer to her as their little sister.

In 2013 we left Australia on our 60-foot custom built catamaran when Sarsha was ten years old. The first obstacle we had to overcome was the toilet training on the boat. Fortunately, I have always taught my dogs to pee on command so when it came to the boat, we took Sarsha up to the front netting and just told her to do 'pee pee'. She walked straight onto the netting squatted and did what was necessary. Later that night we heard the pitter patter of her paws along the deck and then the squeaking of the netting and then a tinkle tinkle into the water. That was the full extent of Sarsha's toilet training on the boat.

During our first month's cruising Sarsha lost a lot of her toy balls overboard. This would happen because when we were playing ball she would get distracted with her guard duties, hearing a noise outside she'd run up on deck then drop the ball to bark at whatever the intrusion was. Obviously, one cannot bark with a ball in one's mouth. She would then stare at her ball, whimpering as it disappeared in the wake of our boat – bye bye ball. However, after going through a number of balls she soon learnt they were not coming back. The loss of her favourite was a tragedy. Then one day we had to laugh. She raced outside with the ball in her mouth and instead of dropping it to bark she held it in her mouth and proceeded with a muffled bark at the same time. We never lost a ball again.

Over time, we all settled into our routines and boat jobs, even Sarsh. Sarsha's primary jobs were to chase the birds off the boat, catch flies, assist Phil in reducing the mosquito population and most importantly of all guard our home from any dubious intruders. She took her guard duties and chores very seriously to the extent she would sometimes grab the fly swat out of my hand to try and do the 'hooman' thing with it but then look at me as if to say, "What do I do now mum?" The guard duty however, was the really important one. We felt we did not need to lock up our boat with Sarsh there to look after it. The other activity that Sarsh would try to help me with was fishing, although I must say that it was not always appreciated. She would get so excited when I grabbed my fishing line and would race up to my favourite fishing spot ahead of me at the bow of the boat, talking to me the whole way there and of course frightening all the fish away. We would both sit up the front side by side staring into the water waiting for the rod to bend. As soon as the tip started to dance up and down so did Sarsh. She was not backwards in coming forward in telling me either, was our Sarsh.

Having Sarsha on the boat just added to our whole boating experience. When you have this special little soul as your companion there are lots of things you do that you would otherwise not do. For example, we often would not have gone ashore in many places but did so for the joy of giving Sarsha a walk. Other times when we were feeling a little lazy Sarsha would ask very politely if we would take her ashore, and of course we did. It was good exercise for everyone. Everything we did, we did with Sarsha in mind. When it came to travelling up the river for a couple of nights in Borneo to see the Orangutans, Sarsha came on the local boat with us too. By the second day, boats coming in the other direction would call out her name and say hello. She replied very exuberantly. The river telegraph had transmitted her name along the length of the river. She became quite a celebrity.

Sarsh was a buddy who loved the simple things in life. She liked nothing more than to swim in the sea, chase fish in the rock pools, and go for walks with us on the beach. Whenever we went to other boats she would often be invited along. People would say, "Make sure you bring Sarsh." Many other boats had left their pets behind and were only too happy to have her aboard for sundowners. They would often say that they needed a 'dog fix'. If we went to a boat and Sarsh was not invited aboard she was happy to sit in the dinghy tied from the back of the boat with her head resting on the dinghy seat looking at the passing scene. As long as she was near to us, she was happy. At one of the anchorages Sarsha was invited along to a children's birthday party. The children came by after lunch and picked her up and had a wonderful afternoon. Sarsha came back all smiles with a party hat around her neck and a bag of goodies for us.

As our sailing years progressed Sarsha became more the old sea dog, getting a little slower in her activities, and a little less able in the hearing department. We had to chide her a few times because there would be the sound of birds twittering in the rigging with Sasha laying around below sunning herself on deck and neglecting her duties. We overlooked this at times because of her hearing deficit and ageing years, but at other times we would catch Sarsha's attention by saying, "Hey Sarsh". She would groggily raise her head then look up as if to say, "What?" We would say incredulously "Birdies!" and she would jump up like a shot and run up along the deck vigorously shouting at the birds to get off her boat. That was our Sarsh.

Time saw Sasha become the well-travelled companion. She came with us to places such as the Spice Islands of Indonesia, Malaysia, Thailand, Sumatra, the Andaman Islands of India, and to see the Orangutans of Borneo. She was young in spirit, but the years were beginning to catch up with her. While we were in Thailand Sarsha became ill, so much so, that we came to the decision to say goodbye, so she would not suffer. We went to our usual vet in Phuket to ask if they would come to our boat to put her out of her suffering. They declined to do so as they were Buddhist and their religion dictated that they not kill anything. This was a real blow to us as we did not want to see her suffer. In the end, we had to do the deed ourselves. Fortunately, our daughter-in-law is a vet and with her knowledge and the help of YouTube we learnt how to administer a catheter and put Sarsh to sleep. That day we lost our friend and companion of 15 years. We could not come to terms with the traditional sea burial and gave Sarsha a resting place under the palm trees on a small island off the coast of Thailand. I understood that day how people must feel when a family member is left behind in another country after a loss of their life fighting a war. It felt like I was leaving Sarsh behind. It was hard for a while, but life and sailing go on. I will always remember that special little companion that brought so many hours of joy and happiness into our lives.

Bio: I am a grandmother of four, traveling around the world with my husband on our custom-built catamaran. We left Australia five years ago with our dog Sarsha. We are presently in Greece. I have a "*Southern Wing*" Face Book page where I record our sailing adventures when we do a voyage. We came from Thailand this year through the Gulf of Aden to the Mediterranean.

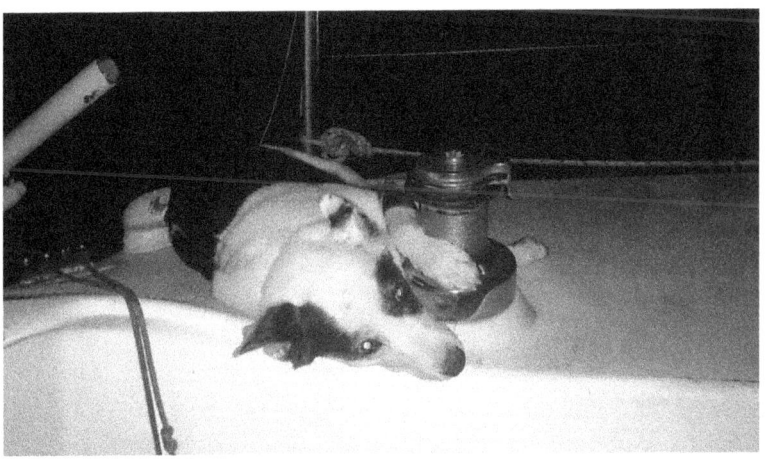

Sarsha on night watch (above)
and admiring the view (over the page) (Sandy Wise)

Lady Nugget takes on the World
by Justine Porter

The plane touched down and I walked to the terminal to see a chocolate ball of fluff with golden brown eyes happily looking out at me. Her journey had been a success. Little did I know that this sweet-tempered Labrador was going to take on the world. That first weekend, she jumped into the utility as we headed into Western Australia's harsh desert bush in search of gold. She adapted well to her new surroundings, helping us dig holes for the gold. The name Nugget was chosen for her, and quickly shortened to Nuggie after the looks we got when people asked her name! Oh, a chocolate nugget, hmm no she's not a poo, she's gold in our eyes!

Nuggie was a quick study and learnt many tricks, sit, lie, and wait. By six months she was playing dead after being 'shot', although the wagging tail for a treat took a little longer to stop (it seems when a dog 'dies' their tail is the last thing to stop beating!). She learnt to shake hands and was terrific when walking alongside with no lead and stopping at roads. Amazingly, after my husband spent time taking her food from her for a few seconds during meals, unlike most labs she ate her food slowly, even stopping to check her surroundings throughout! A trick to behold in a Labrador.

Little did I know this training and fantastic behaviour would open doors to greater things!

When she was a year old, we decided to start working towards a dream of living on the water. A catamaran would be the best option to suit a large dog and we got cracking on the journey of realising this dream.

A move closer to water was required and as a crazy after thought we considered learning how to sail might be a good idea. We had spent many years in the Northern Territory on small fishing boats and had a good understanding of water and weather, but the flapping sails were a mystery to us. Nuggie would have to learn to swap her bush bashing travels with water bobbing adventures!

So off to Nhulunbuy on the remote east Arnhem Land coast it was. We traversed flooded roads with an excited Nuggie who loves the water and travel.

We bought a red polycraft to get us in the water fishing and called it the *Red Barron*. Nuggie was delighted but slightly perplexed at the effort we took to keep her out of the water. As she had spent the first two years of her life swimming in safe waters, she was not aware of the dangers of snapping handbags in these waters. Crocodiles were a real worry, so lessons were needed to be croc smart!

Nuggie took to the boat. This was far better than a car as she sat high and proud encouraging us to go faster, no need to lean her head sideways out the window to get those ears flying and slobber spinning out the back! And this fishing lark was awesome. As the fish came aboard, she would watch intrigued at their flipping, flopping ways, nose sucking in the new smells only to discover much to her delight that they were super tasty. A quick lesson soon followed about waiting for hooks to be removed. She will always carry a small scar on her nose to remind her of her exuberance to snatch a delicious fish too quickly – best to let the dad sort them hooks out first!

Very soon we had the opportunity to learn to sail on *Wombat*, an old 30-foot Van de Stadt that had already taken three trips to the bottom of the ocean. After each rescue she wore the scars of these dastardly trips, no motor, no electrics, and a shabby interior. After assisting the owner to spruce her up a bit, and popping some new rigging on, we decided to see how she sailed. So, our first lesson sailing took place – the owner happy for us to go it alone. As we sailed off the mooring Nuggie found a safe spot, plonked herself down and promptly fell asleep. As the angle of heel increased, she moved to a new spot behind the captain that ensured she was tucked in safely, surveyed the water for potential snacks, determined that we were only coddiwompling and so fell asleep again.

This reassured us that she would be an awesome sailing dog!

She loved *Wombat* and sailing in the bay of Nhulunbuy to the granite islands for nights of sleeping under the stars. On and off the mooring we would take her, watching as we made mistakes, yelled, laughed, googled, and tried new ways and eventually kind of getting it right. Well, we didn't have to sail past the mooring several times to snag it now!

The time came for our 48-foot catamaran *Shima* to be picked up from the Philippines. We took three months off work to sail her home – maybe we should have sailed a catamaran to learn? Oh well it can't be much different.

Nuggie was delighted, she loved new people and a lovely agency nurse, and her partner, took on the role of Nuggie carers. Monica and Jamie usually live in the Austrian mountains in the Fulpmes, they run a backpacker's hostel and often come to Australia as Monica is Australian. They soak up the warmth from our shores away from those cold snowy mountains.

Nuggie approved of our choice immensely and took to long walks on the beach and snuggles. She even snuck onto their bed (not allowed with us, she was thinking these guys are way cooler) and relished bike rides! An active young couple, she was enchanted by their company.

Three months later she stood on the groin outside the Nhulunbuy Yacht Club, high on the rocks looking out to sea and saw a huge white boat sail into the harbour. As we stepped ashore, she nonchalantly wandered over, said hello, got a big cuddle and said, "Stuff that I'm not living in that metal beast, these guys are too cool, can I stay with them?" We said, "Sorry Nuggie they live in the snow on the other side of the planet, you must let them go."

Our sail back had been long and hard, with lots of fun interspersed, but we had been stuck for 10 days with bad weather, not being able to get off the boat. We now had plans to go to many places in Australia that didn't allow dogs and intended to sail in croc-infested waters. Nuggie was six years old and the only 'child' we had, how could we leave her behind? In a dilemma we worried, compiled a pros and cons sheet, talked with friends on big properties to see if maybe they would look after her, but none could. We had offers from people who loved her, but none were suitable owners for our special girl.

Returning from work one day, my heart missed a beat, Nuggie was not sitting on the edge of the grass waiting. There was no fence, but she was so well behaved it wasn't needed, our neighbour reported that she never stepped over the imaginary line. Usually such an obedient girl – where was she? A note was pinned to the door from Monica:

Stolen Nuggie for a walk on beach! Will return later!

As I slept during the day after the night shifts, I would hear this sneaky couple approach and steal her for the day, the love they had for her was gorgeous! Nuggie loved them back and was always on her best behaviour.

One night there was a tentative knock on the door, Monica and Jamie came inside and plonked themselves on the floor rubbing Nuggie's belly and asked the big question, "Can we take Nuggie back to Austria?"

I'm sure she understood as she jumped up and leapt from couch to door in her usual excited fashion then sat at their side begging us to say yes! With tears in our eyes we knew this was an opportunity that couldn't be missed, our gorgeous daughter would be loved and cared for by this awesome couple.

As a sure sign that they were going to give her a fabulous life they refused to send her via normal pet crate and paid the extra money for her to fly with Jet Pets. She received luxury treatment staying at a pet resort during quarantine, where we could Skype her daily, and getting walks at each airport. They arranged her European pet passport and sent us pictures of her wonderful new home!

The day came to take her to the airport, we placed her toys and an Ozzie flag shirt in her crate with a sign for the airport crew that said she loved to be talked to and patted.

I cried and cried as I gave her my final cuddle and saw a tear in Glen's eye too. She looked a little forlorn but settled down to snooze as soon as we walked away – she loved travelling, no worries there!

I cried for weeks after, the silence in the house was very painful, I knew in my heart she would have a better and safer life than I could offer her on a boat, in croc-infested waters, but still my heart was broken. It was the hardest choice we have ever had to make, but we made it for her best interests not ours.

Her arrival to Austria was smooth and the first photos came streaming in – Nuggie with her thankfully thick chocolate coat snuffling in the snow, climbing the hills, chasing new doggie friends. We read hostel.com posts with reviews from backpackers talking of it being the best place to stay and Nuggie the dog being the highlight! Our hearts lifted as videos of her ice skating, sledging, and running amok in the snow started pouring in. Monica told me she adapted so well to the cold she actually seemed younger now she wasn't stifled by the tropical heat of Nhulunbuy. She would jump into the freezing waters and swim to her heart's content. Frolicking and rolling in the snow now her favourite pastime!

Her doggie passport started filling with new places as she did weekend trips all over Europe.

We realised we really had made a superb choice. Over time we had to let her go from our hearts and recognise Monica and Jamie as her new parents, this really was quite a hard thing. I still miss her dreadfully and while writing her story I have had a tear or two. Reading it out to my hubby, I watched as he shed a tear too, she is still locked in our hearts! We will always be her first parents.

I think Nuggie still has thoughts of being on a boat. A while back she was running around with her best doggie friend and misjudged the ice, sliding with a thwack into his side. She yelped but continued to play. By that evening she was rubbing her eye. Her astute new parents took her straight to the vet but alas she had a velocity injury to her eye. Over many weeks of trying to stop the damage it was realised that the eye could not be saved and it was removed. So now Nuggie is a doggy pirate with just one eye. It has not slowed her down at all – maybe, just maybe, she really wanted to be a boat dog after all!

Bio: Justine and Glen had their dream boat built in the Philippines and sailed her home in 2014. They gave up their ties to land the following year to sail and explore Australia's least known places. Self-taught sailors with a love of sea but no sailing experience they have close to 10,000 nm under their belts. They plan to add many more miles, finding creatures to play with along the way to alleviate the missing pets in their lives!

Nugget's new home

Nugget (Justine Porter)

The Reluctant Adventures of Hastings: A Boat Dog's Tale
by Lucy Wilcox Claiborne

Dear Fellow, Furry Beast,

Let me introduce myself. I am Captain Hastings, a furry quadruped, and superior beast of the sailing vessel *Independence*. Not that I had any choice in the purchase and commissioning of my vessel. It was simply thrust upon me. And then, the 'adventures' began. I write to you, Fellow Furry Beast, so you can be alert and watch for the signs of an impending sailing adventure.

You may be napping in the sun, or enjoying a chicken dinner, or rolling in skunk pee, and then, disaster will strike. I, myself, was preparing for elevenses when the ordeal began. My friends, '*a plan*' had been enacted.

These Humans are feebleminded, so, in order to come up with 'a plan', they spend lots of time 'building spreadsheets' and 'saving money'. Be on your guard if they start eating food out of tins. If your Humans stay home staring at you on Friday nights, this is a bad sign. If they post pictures of fiberglass death traps floating on a turbulent sea, this is a bad sign. I foolishly assumed they were saving money to avoid ever having to live on this torture device, the sure fate of only the poorest, most wretched creatures. I was wrong.

One day, we departed our normal abode. Presumably, for a better abode, with a bigger Large Cold Food Device and a better Cold Air Machine. My confusion started when we approached the infamous fiberglass death trap, named *Independence*. Independence from sanity, obviously. The in-person manifestation of what I thought was an artist's rendering designed to be a cautionary tale for the most wayward. OK, I get it. I'll put off the howling for dinner until 5 pm instead of 4:45 pm. I will be a better beast!

My howls of despair and confusion did nothing to dampen their enthusiasm. They seemed happy to the point of distraction. I then heard the Humans say, "Home again, home again, jiggedy jig". Home again? Home should have a Large Cold Food Device! Full power Cold Air Machines! It shouldn't be this dreadful place! What is to become of me? I fell into a distracted sleep and dreamed of eating chicken and sitting in cold air. Then I woke up. On *Independence*. Surrounded by a sea of trouble. And the Humans said, "Let's go on an adventure".

The only thing to do was to settle in for an ordeal. The word adventure should mean liberating underappreciated chicken from the dinner table. However, my misguided Humans use it to describe ordeals such as sitting on hot, food-less beaches, reading boring interpretive signs, and looking at other animals that live in the sea and are useless. These tribulations rarely feature edible elevenses, lunches, or after lunch snacks, adding to my deep and unyielding affliction.

It goes without saying that I, a furry quadruped, like land. Land is good. Land is the best pee-station. Let me teach you the most important lesson of all: give up on land. If your humans put you on a boat, life as you know it is over. Forget about land. Go ahead and pee on the boat.

It was an easy decision for me. The boat moved across the water. Time passed. I had to remind the Humans about dinner. During an unnecessary and loud yelling event known as anchoring, the boat stopped. From here, I could smell land again. I could see land. I already knew these Humans were incapable of getting me to said land, so, I peed on the deck. Then, instead of rewarding me for my ingenuity, they punished me by placing me into an even more dreadful Smaller Death Trap, called a dinghy. They started the mechanical device for moving the dinghy which promptly died. They engaged their weak and puny muscles and attempted to row. There was yelling and crying. It was dark. I was howling in despair. You must know that we never set foot on land that night. We made it back to *Independence*, which seemed nice in comparison. They noticed the pee. Yes, foolish humans, I had given up on you long before. There was no need of the additional adventure/ordeal.

Dear Fellow Furry Friends, this is my advice to you: just give up. Your Humans might be as incompetent as mine. This is your sad, sorry life now. Get used to it. Pee on the deck.

"Exciting news! We are ready for the next adventure!" Just when you think life can't get any worse, it suddenly does. We departed the sight of land. We rocked from side to side. We bounced up and down. The wind howled and made everything clank. Everything creaked. No one could walk or think or move. It got dark. We kept going. The wind kept howling. The darkness got darker. I lay down in despair and dreamt of chicken.

I woke up to silence. Land? Yes! It must be! Land! A Human got off the boat. I produced myself, ready to check out this strange new land of 'landiness'. No, you must wait. We must "show papers" first. Dear Fellow, Furry Beast, Humans like tribulations. First, they must show the white square things to other humans, along with smaller green bits of paper. I'd understand if they had to make a peace offering of chicken, but nope, these Humans are obsessed with paper. If you want to find out how much they love paper, just eat some smaller green bits. Then you'll see.

After the paper debacle, we get in the dinghy. Just between you and me, once you get used to this uncivilized conveyance, the dinghy is actually OK. But don't tell the Humans this. The Humans point out things, "Look, dolphins! Look! Sting Rays! Look! A shark!"

"Look, Humans, all of these creatures are 1) useless, 2) might want to take my precious rations, and 3) are not me." Why do they insist on looking at other creatures when they have me, the most handsome, most useful furry beast to ever live? Humans, they are un-understandable.

We fell into a routine. I found that I could walk around the deck and find a good spot where, instead of my beloved Cold Air Machine, I could find a cool breeze. This cool breeze has the hint of fishiness, which is OK. It would be better if it carried an aroma of chicken, but hey, baby steps. "Let's go on an adventure,", they say. I check the clock. While I have had a satisfactory breakfast, if we go on an ordeal now, there's a strong possibility of missing elevenses. Then, it's just a snowball affair: missing lunch, second lunch, mid-afternoon snack, tea-time, dinner, second dinner, and third dinner. Delaying any opportunity to avail yourself of life-giving sustenance is a very foolish endeavor and is not to be countenanced. "Fine," they say. "We'll go without you." The dinghy is readied. I want to hold my ground, yet I know how foolish they are and how easily lost they get. I need them to return to open the cold food box. I must go with them, regardless of the risks.

We walk. I find the trail. They pull me down the wrong trail and get lost. I pull them down the correct trail. We look at a big, useless, lake of water. I despair. I find a cave with mud. Caves are good. They are cold and dark and stinky and have mud, mud, glorious mud! Concern over elevenses mounts. The Humans sense my un-ease and offer me vile weeds. They think it's funny, but, believe me, it's not. I lead them back to the dinghy. It's not there. Apparently, in my hunger-weakened state, we ended up on the wrong beach. We swim to the right beach, find the dinghy, return to *Independence*. I assist the Humans in opening the Cold Food Machine and eat everything I can. Don't tell the Humans, but sometimes, adventures are OK.

"Let's go on an adventure." It's awfully close to dinner time, I infer by angrily hitting my empty dinner bowl. "It will be fun," they say. Sigh. I jump in the dinghy. We arrive at a boardwalk. I see land; I see a beautiful grassy meadow. I leap off the boardwalk and to my shock and horror, it's wet and cold. My legs are doggy-paddling. Where is the land, sweet land? "Silly you! That's not land, it's just floating, green duckweed." I am lifted up, placed on the boardwalk, wet, humiliated, deceived.

Dear Fellow Furry Friends, deception is all around you. Duckweed floating on water can look like land. Humans will try and offer you vile weeds and yuck berries as food sources. Sometimes, adventures are ordeals. Sometimes, ordeals, properly leveraged by wily beasts like myself, are opportunities for extra sympathy rations.

One day the Humans got bored with their innumerable patent pending torture devices. "I know," they say, "Let's go on an adventure!" A Somehow Even Smaller Death Trap is produced. What fresh hell? I am handed on to this very unstable device, clearly not suitable for living beings. It's certainly not designed to carry two humans and one furry beast. I protest. I am, customarily, ignored, and passed onto the paddle board. Wet water laps over us. With every forward stroke, death by drowning is imminent. And yet, we arrive on land. We swim in the sea. We sniff out crabs and shells. And we make it home, just in time for first dinner.

Sometimes, wondrous events happen. We dock *Independence*. We walk the streets. Very friendly, wonderful, and wise humans come up to me and give me the appreciation I deserve.

"Are you a Cocker Spaniel?"
"Yes."
"Would you like a treat?"
"Yes."

Life can be so sweet when you are properly appreciated. We travel for miles in this area, and every new town is full of cocker spaniel appreciating people. I have found me a home.

"Furry Beast, there is a hurricane. Don't worry, we'll stay. We just might not have Cold Air or Large Cold Food Device."

"Dear humans, can we go somewhere there is Cold Air and Large Cold Food Devices?"

"Yes."

Well, dear humans, that is the obvious choice! We leave. We go to a place on solid ground with a Large Food Device and Cold Air. It's hard to admit. It's hard to explain. But I didn't like it. These long halls and big spaces are hard to supervise all humans from. It's hard to get comfy. The air doesn't smell of fish. I miss my home. I miss my adventures. We watch video of *Independence*, holding on and bouncing in her dock. The video cuts out as the wind and surge mount. Despair follows. Elevenses are consumed every hour.

And then, it's over. We go home. *Independence* is less of a death trap than I thought. You never know how strong something is until it's tested. You never know how much fun ordeals can be until they are threatened. I step aboard. Home again, home again, jiggedy jig.

And so, my dear Fellow Furry Beast, what should you do if you are forced into an ill-conceived ordeal? I say: Pack your elevenses. Best paw forward. Let's go on an adventure.

Yours sincerely,
Captain Hastings
S/V *Independence*

Bio: Lucy lives on her 38-foot sailboat. She travels with her husband and dog in the eastern U.S. and the Bahamas while working remotely. She enjoys drinking tea, eating chocolate, and planning adventures for her dog, Hastings.

Pet Bio: Captain Hastings, a proud furry quadruped of the Cocker Spaniel variety, has been offering expert supervision to his hapless humans for 13 years. He has been chief nourishment officer on the sailing vessel *Independence* for the last four years. He has travelled thousands of miles through the eastern U.S. and the Bahamas and has never missed a meal.

Hastings with Lucy (Lucy Wilcox Claiborne)

The Big Decision
by Carolyn Wasik

My official name is Magnolia May Petersen. I am known as Maggie May to most of my friends and I am a one-hundred-pound Golden Retriever. I wanted to get that out-front right away. I have lived with Carolyn (a human) and her husband (also a human) for seven years; they are my fourth owners, not through any fault of my own.

I have been able to observe humans closely over the years and have deduced that they are basically very unsatisfied beings. They appear to always be searching for that elusive 'something' that will make them happy. Canines are more evolved and understand that this is it; we live in the here and now, and to be frank, my here and now was just perfect. You noticed I said 'was' that's because it was just about to change.

I had been lying in bed with Carolyn while she read some magazine that had a sailboat on the front with a lady waving and holding a little pooch. You know the kind of dog all the millennials are carrying around in their Prada bags. I can't read so I didn't think much of it until Gert walked into the room.

"Wow look at this, living on a sailboat and cruising in the Caribbean, the dream life," said Carolyn.

Gert grabbed the magazine and looked at the cover. "Yeah looks great, they even took their dog."

I begged to differ, that creature could hardly be called a dog. It looked like a dust mop.

Gert said, "You know we've talked of this before and you always came up with some excuse as to why we couldn't do it. We could be livin' the dream too. We're not getting any younger and for once we're in a financial position to maybe take off for a few years."

I rolled over, scratching my belly. I've heard this talk before, it ain't happening. Carolyn would never subject me to living on a sailboat; not that I haven't sailed before. There is nothing like laying in the cockpit of their boat *Lucy* (named after their first golden retriever) on a breezy hot day in August. Sailing the Great South Bay on Long Island with friends and snacks all day and belly rubs from humans who loved me, was as close to heaven as it gets. This living aboard sounded a lot different.

The next morning as I rolled off my down comforter, I heard them talking again about this 'cruising' thing, 'liveaboard' stuff. It didn't sound all that great to me. They talked of going to exotic places, eating native foods, experiencing different cultures. Remember I told you that Carolyn and Gert's place was my fourth home? I'd had enough of different cultures. I saw 'trouble'. Besides I was five years old, that is thirty-five in human years, by the time these two got it together I calculated I would be close to seventy; not a good time for life changes.

They had a boat, not big but nice for day sailing; could they really be thinking of taking that little thing? I noticed lately when we went to West Marine they would walk out with big bags of stuff. I didn't understand what this stuff was for, but I heard words like GPS, self-furling, depth sounder, fish finder, radio; my head was whirling. Books and magazines started arriving and though I can't read I just knew they were about this liveaboard life. One day a box was delivered and in it was this strange pot they called a pressure cooker. Carolyn was thrilled. "Look Gert, the pamphlet says it is the only way to cook after you've been awake for three days in a storm and you want something to eat that was quick and easy to make."

Three days in a storm. I moaned, my stomach felt queasy already. Rolling seas, storms. Where was the next Petco store? Or was I supposed to eat that slop out of that pressure cooker contraption?

I had no-one to consult; I didn't know any other dogs who had been to sea. It just didn't seem like the right environment for a canine. We belong on terra firma. The closest I cared to get to fish was when it was in a can.

Which leads me to something else. Swimming. What if I fell overboard in those rough seas they talked about? The next time we went to West Marine I was going to have to take a closer look at safety stuff for dogs. Although I liked to swim, dogs are not known to be able to swim long distances. Most people don't know this, because all they ever do is throw a stick from the beach and yell fetch. The only reason I ever went in and brought the stick back was because I knew there was a treat waiting when I returned. I will do almost anything for a treat. The whole idea of floating in the water wearing some kind of flotation device gave me the creeps. My paws would look like appetizers to sharks. I was starting to have nightmares; my body twitched even when I laid down for my naps.

Which raises another point, when I'm not sleeping, I like to play. We go out every day; either to the park or to the beach. I like to keep my weight at around a hundred pounds but to do this I must exercise. Their boat was twenty-eight feet long; not a lot of room to run. I heard talk of being out to sea for weeks on end. WEEKS ON END!

Here's a big one, bathroom duties. I am very private, always seeking the areas where I can pee and poop alone. I didn't see anywhere on this boat that was private and clearly no grass or dirt to scratch in. Carolyn started walking me around the boat on a leash and then she would stop usually on the foredeck and squat and make these ridiculous sounds; I realized she was trying to mimic someone going to the bathroom. She looked ridiculous and I did not go to the bathroom.

I started to pant with anxiety when I overheard the word 'quarantine'. It appears certain countries do not let animals set foot on their land without being caged for a certain amount of time, something to do with disease. I have never set foot in a cage, despite all the doggy literature of how it makes dogs feel safe – a return to their cave days. I have no desire to return to some primitive state. As I said, I sleep on a down comforter – there are no bars and I felt perfectly safe.

I stopped eating. I lost weight. This was the only way I knew to communicate how I felt. Carolyn worried and took me to my holistic vet. He wanted to know if anything was different in our home. Carolyn proceeded to tell him of their plans. "Well that's it for Pete's sake. She doesn't want to go, she's depressed," the vet said. At last someone was listening to me. I rolled my big brown eyes towards Carolyn giving the classic "hang dog" look.

When we got home, she fixed my favorite meal and then tucked me into their bed. The door closed, and I jumped out of bed and put my ear against it. I heard them talking. I was sure it was about me. Maybe they were coming to their senses. I went back to bed and nuzzled under the comforter certain they would make the only sensible decision.

Well they made a decision alright. As it turned out they decided to not take me with them. I was shocked and hurt. Now I really was depressed. I continued my hunger strike, well just for another day. They attempted to buy my love. My favorite foods, a doggie massage. The vet put me on some anti-depression medication. I figured I might as well play this one to the hilt; but I am resilient, I believe all dogs are as we are subject to human whims. I decided if this was their choice, they had better leave me with the only person I loved more than Carolyn. That was her sister Vivian. Aunt Vivian and Uncle John had a sheep farm with three dogs, and two cats, plus their two children Katie and John who loved me. They were smart enough to stay on land with their animals.

They did finally decide to leave me on the farm. I was annoyed at first but in the end felt this was the best decision. Carolyn kept hugging and crying as she left me telling me it was only going to be for a year or so.

The end result was they were gone for close to five years. I had a great time on the farm and didn't have nightmares anymore about drowning, rough seas, crappy food, QUARANTINE. Life was good.

The sad part of this story is I died while they were away, kidney disease. This was hard on everyone.

It's a big decision to have your dog on board on an extended cruise, especially an older dog. I hope that when you are considering this you will glance back over my story and consider the pros and cons. What you want as a human may not be what your dog prefers.

Bio: Carolyn Wasik-Petersen is a retired teacher and social worker. She and her husband are making a move from New York to North Carolina where they have built their home on the Intracoastal Waterway. The Intracoastal holds special memories as it was here that Carolyn's sailing adventures began. Carolyn is a farm girl from Upstate New York whose only contact with water was an old cow pond; however, her husband is Danish and has sailed since a boy. Together they have sailed for close to thirty years from Maine to the South Pacific. Carolyn's other love is dogs. She has had a golden retriever in her life almost all the years she has been married; most were content to sleep by a warm fireplace and not on a rocking sailboat.

Pet Bio: Maggie May was a rescue from Virginia. We were in fact her fourth owners. When I researched her previous owners, the stories went like this: Owner # 1 Maggie was given to an older woman as a gift thinking the woman needed a companion. The woman it turns out didn't want a companion or a dog. She left Maggie to fend for herself locked in a pen, feeding her sporadically. Maggie went up for sale almost immediately. Owner #2 had just had a baby and all her friends told her a child should grow up with a dog preferably a golden retriever. That woman bought Maggie, not because she was beautiful but because she felt sorry for her. She was skinny and sickly looking, which in fact she was. The woman spent the next six months working with a vet to get Maggie back to health. The woman said she thought Maggie was cute playing with (and pulling apart) her daughter's stuffed animals. She didn't think it was cute when Maggie proceeded to rip apart all her flower beds that Spring. Up went the "dog for sale" signs. Owner # 3 A family in Virginia whose thirteen-year-old "perfect" Golden had died a year before took Maggie, I guess thinking all Goldens were "perfect". Their dog brought in the newspaper, fetched their slippers, walked off leash. This was not Maggie May. We became owners #4.

Maggie May with Carolyn (previous page) and art by Carolyn (Carolyn Wasik)

Please Remove DOG
by Rosa Linda Román

The mat normally reads, 'Please Remove Shoes', and sits on the dock beside our boat as a friendly reminder to our guests. But when I approached the *Dawn Treader* one evening there was a piece of paper stuck to the mat that read: 'DOG.'

There, on the deck about six feet above this mat, my sweet girl Nala sat eagerly awaiting my return. At first, I thought someone had stuck the note to my boat to warn people that there was a large German Shepherd on board and the paper had fallen off and landed on the mat. But then it hit me, the sign-maker was being snarky. They placed it exactly where they had intended so that the mat now read, 'Please Remove DOG'.

At that realization I got that hot-all-over, flush-faced feeling that comes from being confronted by your neighbor. Only there was no confrontation. Just this passive-aggressive note, which really wasn't aggressive at all. It was actually a bit clever. Plus, I knew my dog could scare the heck out of people if she wanted to and apparently, while I took my husband an hour away to the Ft. Lauderdale airport and then did some IKEA shopping, she very much wanted to.

Knowing I would be gone for several hours I had left her out on deck deliberately and left the door open to the main cabin area so that she could come in and out as she pleased and use her fake grass potty on the forward deck if she needed to. But as I held this computer-printed DOG sign that night I realized that that had been a mistake. Hindsight may be 20-20, but it didn't help me answer the question of what to do now that the damage was done. And by 'damage' I mean that she upset the neighbors by barking at them whenever they walked by the boat. This was her territory and it was her job to protect us. I knew that she would never jump off and attack anyone. But I tried to put myself in their shoes and remember that they had no way of knowing this as they walked by.

That night I spent hours agonizing about what to do in response. It bothered me that they had gone to the trouble of creating this sign on their computer and printing it on their printer instead of just talking to me, especially since they were one of only two other boats on our dock. I thought of employing their tactic and changing the sign to, 'Please remove... yourself from your high horse!' But I knew when this sweet puppy started barking at someone it could be very scary on the receiving end. The dockhand who collects the garbage generally refers to her as, 'Cujo.' I am fine with that, especially now that our boat is back in this particular slip, at this particular marina. Not only is it on a dead-end dock where there should be no foot-traffic after hours, but it was in that very spot several months earlier that two men had boarded our boat in the middle of the night and tried to rob us.

We were all sound asleep onboard and it was terrifying. At the time Nala was a small puppy in a crate, unaware of these bad men on deck and the potential nightmare they could've caused. Although the men ended up running away when we flipped on the deck light and started yelling, it was not before they had stolen a neighboring boat's instrument panel and electronics. Police were called, the kids were scared, and it wasn't until about an hour later that security wandered over to see what had happened.

So, I'm okay with 'Cujo.' Nala is a deterrent to anyone that might get the same idea, which is good for all the boats on our dock. But the DOG-sign neighbors weren't there when this burglary happened. They are new to the neighborhood. To them Nala is nothing more than a nuisance. Nothing more than a DOG.

After a very restless night's sleep I finally settled on my response. Getting up before dawn the next morning I took their 'DOG' sign and went to work. Thanks to boatschooling three kids, we also have a printer onboard, so I used it to print a few choice words of my own. The end result read:

DOG is sorry.
(Owner too!)
Please forgive us!

As I stepped back to inspect the mat Nala was once again lying directly above it on deck. With her furry face resting on her paws it seemed to me that her expression said, "I really AM sorry!"

Despite our apologetic sign (and later face-to-face apologies, as well) the neighbors never openly softened. No smiles or friendly morning waves as you would normally find between other liveaboards. Walks to and from the boat with Nala are still awkward at best.

But I have to admit the DOG sign was an important wake-up call for me and prompted me to spend a ton of extra time with her, teaching her when it was time to bark and when she should simply watch the person walking by. It helped that this whole thing happened while my kids were out of town (visiting cousins in Chicago) so that I had the time to give her the extra attention. It also gave me the encouragement I needed to start kayaking with Nala to nearby Peanut Island for a run together (rather than risk getting dirty looks walking by on the dock). This extra training time in the kayak ("Sit! Stay! No, don't jump out and swim to shore!") and on those runs definitely helped, too.

In the end I am grateful for the DOG sign incident as I am now a better boat dog mommy because of it; more mindful of continuing her training every day. Plus, I am filled with gratitude that ours is a mobile home. Although this situation wasn't a major neighbor battle by any stretch, if it had gotten ugly, we could just sail away in search of fairer, dog-friendlier harbors.

For me, that newfound freedom is nothing to bark at!

Bio: Rosa Linda Román ("Rosa Linda") is a TV News veteran who left mainstream media to become a fulltime mom in 2005. In 2007 she launched New Mexicast, the first video podcast in the state of New Mexico. Through New Mexicast, Rosa Linda shares enchanting stories about people and places in New Mexico and on her family's many travels, including life aboard the sailing catamarans, *Hakuna Matata* and *Dawn Treader* with three kids and a German Shepherd. Rosa Linda is currently landlocked in Austin, Texas where she is writing a memoir about her family's liveaboard adventures.

Pet Bio: Nala is a 2½ year old German Shepherd who grew up on the sailing catamaran, *Dawn Treader* (a Lagoon 450). Nala loves to swim and lives for shredding coconuts and chasing balls. Nala is famous (infamous?) in George Town, Exuma, Bahamas for having escaped her sitters and taking over Stocking Island for several weeks while her family was away. She has sailed in Florida and the Bahamas and has traveled to more than 25 states with her pack of five humans.

www.NewMexicast.com

Nala (Rosa Linda Román)

Hudson "THE boat dog"
by Kym Phillips

They said, "Get a boat dog!" They said, "It would be fun." And it is!

I'm writing this on his birthday! Hudson Fysh Phillips – what a title... what a mouthful...

Things to know about Hudson. This is his oath:

I Hudson, do not sleep outside on the open deck. I sleep inside the cabin in between my humans, in the middle of the bed. Wet, dry, or otherwise. I am THE boat dog!

I am an extravert. I love people... and new things. And especially new places. I keep the boat safe. I am THE boat dog!

I Hudson, promise to be loving, protective, funny, and loyal... but particularly funny. I am THE boat dog!

I Hudson, eat anything and EVERYTHING. I am THE boat dog!

I Hudson, require undivided attention, long runs on the beach, lots of swimming, and a good movie to watch when the weather is unpleasant. I am THE boat dog!

I Hudson, do not understand the word 'can't.' This word does not exist.

I Hudson, love the tender... the faster it goes the better. I am THE boat dog!

I Hudson, do not 'do' alone... and somebody will pay if I am left in this state!

The following is one of our many stories:

We have lived aboard for almost twelve months. Looking for a companion that was smallish in size and robust, we spent hours trying to find a breed of dog that was suitable. Then we found the Cairn Terrier. Hardy, fearless, assertive, intelligent, active, happy – this breed sounded perfect to us. 'Toto' from the Wizard of Oz was a Cairn Terrier!

Hudson was seven weeks old when we picked him up and introduced him to his new home – the boat! We were nervous. Would this work? It was a big commitment. What if he got seasick? We cut pool noodles up and shoved them into every hole, scupper, and fairlead. He soon worked out that fake turf was as good as real grass. Fender ropes became floppy sticks that must be wrestled. Everyone on a boat or beach was his friend – even if they weren't.

As cruisers know, we meet many wonderful people along our way and bump into people we haven't seen for many years. While were in Mackay, Queensland, we met up with a guy who my Dear Husband (DH) played football with 30 years ago. Well you can imagine what happened. We started with a beer and lunch, a few beers, a few more beers, then dinner, and a couple of rums.

From the pub, during the course of the afternoon we could see Hudson sitting up on "watch" at the bow of the boat from where we were sitting, everything was great! Or so we thought. The pub closed, and we said goodbye to our friends.

This was Hudson's first time left alone for an extended period. He was always fine for a couple of hours while we did the shopping, what could possibly go wrong? Well, it turns out he's frightened of the dark! This big brave dog of ours – THE boat dog (fearless they said).

Our boat was 800 metres from the entry to the marina facilities. It couldn't be further away if we'd tried. It's a long walk when the beer/rum monster has had you in his pocket all day. Many bevies later we returned to the boat. The aircon was running, Hudson had dog chews, toys, TV was on, and a bowl full of dog biscuits.

We climbed onboard, usually Hudson would be there to greet us. No dog! Open the saloon dog. No dog! My heart was sinking.

The guilt, I shouldn't have left him, I wanted to come back and check on him, but DH had said that he was fine, he's a dog.

Into the saloon. No dog. I called and called. No dog. My heart was racing, I started to perspire, I was sure he'd gone overboard. I checked the heads, flybridge. No dog. I was just reaching for the spotlight when I heard, "Oh f#@* Hudson – you've done it this time – you're in big trouble..."

I swung open the main cabin door. I was disorientated for a moment, I couldn't understand what I was looking at. Oh, my goodness... the mess. It looked like a million little ducklings had exploded. Hudson had dug his way into our bed. Two mattress toppers and the mattress destroyed. All you could see were two little ears. I cannot explain in words how horrendous the site was. Blue foam, white foam, feathers, torn sheets, ripped doona.

My DH, in his current state, was laughing so hard. He said, "Oh it's not that bad... my side is fine," and promptly fell on the bed asleep. If there was ever a point in my life that I could have snapped that was it!

Of course, we forgave Hudson, apologised for leaving him alone so long, gave him a kiss, and threw him outside onto the back deck.

The new 'no-go' cabin zone went on for a couple of nights, so he could work out that what he did was wrong, wrong, wrong (intelligent they said). He was banned from sleeping in our bed, in the morning he could come in for a cuddle... until, day five post-mattress-incident, (assertive they said).

Our morning ritual is to jump out of bed, do the usual anchor, lines, location checks, make the coffee, and pick up the crossword book. This particular morning, I needed my reading glasses to complete the crossword and guess what.... Yep you guessed it, they were missing. The hunt began. Hudson was cowering in the corner with a small piece of pink looking substance in the fur under his chin. Oh nooooooo! My glasses. There they were on the floor – only one wing remained, one smashed frame and no glass. ANYWHERE! He had chewed the glass. Panic! Four tins of sardines became the 'glass bait'. This in turn created a loose shiny shimmering poo (hardy they said).

To date he hasn't eaten another bed, but we also haven't left him alone in the dark. He sleeps between the humans in the middle of the bed and this saves us a fortune on optical wear. We are well trained humans now. We go, he goes! (active and happy they said).

This year he has travelled over 2,000 nautical miles. Not a bad life for THE boat dog!

He's the best friend any girl could have! (So they said)!

Bio: Kym is a recently retired professional who has performed roles anywhere from teaching veterinary nursing through to 11 years as Commercial Manager for Australia's largest privately-owned forestry management company. Kym has taken to the water on board *Miss McKinlay* (50-foot Clipper Cordova) with her husband and trusty boat dog Hudson Fysh. She maintains a Facebook page *"Miss McKinlay"* where she keeps track of their travels.

Hudson (Kym Phillips)

Ivy's Escape
by Lanise Edwards

We were well overdue to haul *Easter Rose* out of the water for antifouling and maintenance. The last time this expensive chore was completed we stayed in a holiday house for three days. This time, with three weeks of hard work ahead of us, we decided to stay onboard. Fortunately, the boatyard in Bundaberg had actual steps rather than a ladder, which made access to the boat possible. A ladder was not going cut it for myself or Ivy our old Labrador.

The steps were steep and initially Ivy refused to climb them as she could see the ground beneath, this unnerved her. After some consideration we tied shade cloth underneath the steps. Ivy was happy to walk up and down with us following and holding her lead. With that hurdle overcome we began a daily routine of sanding and grinding to prepare the hull for a thorough paint and overhaul. Ivy spent most of her days on a lead sleeping in the cool shade of the boat or on deck as we worked on *Easter Rose*.

After 10 days on the hardstand Ivy had a good routine and waited for us to escort her down the steps for her morning walk. I guess I became comfortable and secure in the knowledge that Ivy would not attempt the steps alone. I should have known her better. In hindsight it was very likely she had been scheming her 'great escape' for several days! This is Ivy's style, and I underestimated her tenacity and cunning.

One morning I woke early, let Ivy off her lead in the cockpit and ventured back below decks to prepare a well-earned coffee. Still in my mismatched PJs I eventually came back on deck with coffee in hand, noticing Ivy was not in the cockpit. Aching all over from the previous day's hard work and noticing last night's shower had not removed residue paint from my hands and feet, I glanced around. Still no sign of Ivy. Surely, she was not brave enough to go down the steps alone? I was mistaken.

As my foggy morning-brain stepped up a gear, I knew I had to act quickly. Our old Labrador was more than capable of sneaking off once my guard was down. And it was. Ivy could not have chosen a worse time! My antifoul splattered body and odd pyjamas looked a sight, not to mention my knotted hair also sprinkled with primer and other paint residue.

There was no time to waste, with a busy road out the front and miles of river and esplanade, not to mention trucks and workmen with forklifts. Ivy could be in danger and oblivious to it. I bolted down the steps without further thought and paced around the large yard peering in every corner. No sign of Ivy. Surely, she could not have gone far? How long had she been gone? I had no idea. I figured it was early and no one would be around, so I chanced running out onto the road in my PJs. I noticed some workman on the road and asked if they had seen a black Labrador. They glanced at me slightly oddly, I obviously didn't realise how I looked. They both pointed, stating that she had gone one of two different directions. I was confused and had to take a guess which direction she would head. This meant crossing the road and walking to the esplanade pathway. I scanned up and down and kept calling her name in an increasingly loud, agitated manner, as I became aware that the world was waking up and people (normally-dressed people!) were appearing.

Too late to return to the boat, I forged on. Finally, in the far distance I spotted a black dog near the seafood co-op skip bins. This had to be Ivy. Ivy loves a rotten smell to investigate! I ran back to the road and towards the co-op. Now many people were present. Some just stared. I must have looked like a madwoman on a mission, covered in weird blue paint with war-like smears of silver primer on my face and in my hair. My mismatched PJs, lack of a bra, and crazed look must have topped it off. I yelled to Ivy as I could see it was definitely her. She froze, and I thought my search was over.

Ivy glanced around, then turned her back to me as if she had no clue who I was and could not hear me. Her hearing is acute; however, she had no intention of stopping or responding. By now I was a woman possessed, frustrated and cranky. I scolded her from a distance and demanded that she, "Come now!" I was infuriated. My voice obviously loud, people enjoying a relaxing morning coffee at the cafe stared. Beyond embarrassment at this point, I was hellbent on catching Ivy before she ate some gruesome morsel of rotten seafood that would result in a very messy aftermath!

I ran quickly towards her, approaching the bins as Ivy snorted, sniffed and kept chewing something revolting on the ground. Still completely ignoring me, she was obviously obsessed with her find. I took advantage and cornered her. Once an arm's length away Ivy looked up at me as if to say; "Oh I didn't see you, what's the problem?" Grimacing I attached her lead and pulled her away from the bins. I had her in my grips and she acted as if she did not have a clue why I was angry or what the drama was!

I marched her back down the road, appearing like an abusive crazy dog owner as I muttered more than a few expletives under my breath. By this time the road was busy, workmen and boatyard staff had arrived. Yachties and locals were strolling by the café, enjoying their morning walks. I wished I could have shrunk into the asphalt as I became excessively aware of my PJ-clad appearance. I trudged back to the boatyard with Ivy.

Entering the yard people were out working on boats. I held my head high and picked up my pace towards *Easter Rose*, shoving Ivy up the steps and collapsing in the cockpit. It was then that the humourous side of my morning hit me and I began to laugh hysterically. Emerging from the cockpit my husband asked where I had been. I rolled my eyes and replied, "Oh just for a walk!"

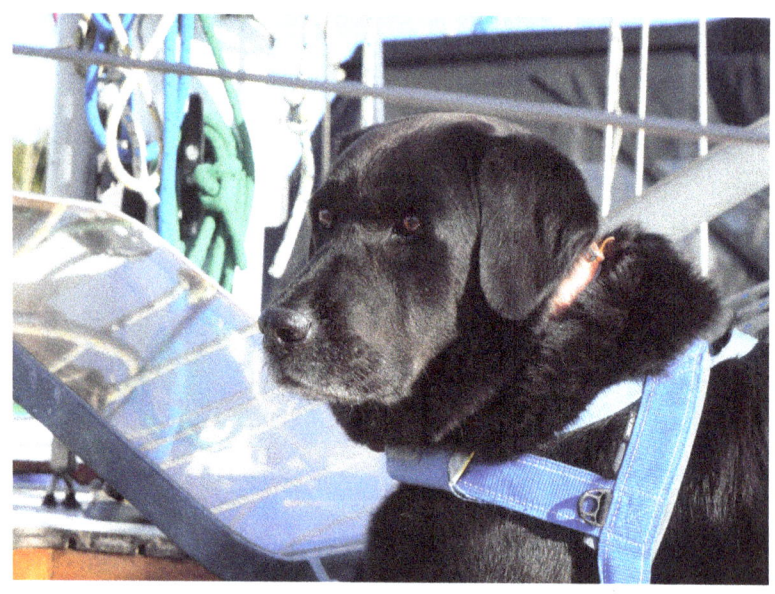

Ivy (Lanise Edwards)

PART TWO: CURIOUS CATS

Listy the Barge Cat
by Jane Chevoux

I didn't start out as a barge cat. Mum and her human kitten, Jon, lived in a little cottage behind the high street when they adopted me. It had a tiny back yard with a well and garden shed I could hide under and a tree-ship Mum built for Jon and me to climb. I got lonely when Jon went to school so they adopted a kitten brother for me, we called him Obi from Jon's favourite film. My name is Lister, after the cool space adventurer in his favourite TV show, *Red Dwarf.*

Obi and I used to watch out of the window for Mum and Jon to come home then race through the cat flap to meet them. When they went shopping, I would follow and sit at the corner of the alley behind the grog shop, calling loudly so they wouldn't get lost. It's important to look after your humans like that.

One day they packed everything up in boxes and put Obi and me in our travelling basket. We walked over the road, across the railway track, past the boatyard and along the river wall to where a wooden path on stilts went 50 yards out over the mud. At the end of this was a plank leading down to a green steel barge. "Welcome aboard your new home," Mum said.

Nooit Volmaakt is a Dutch sailing barge of a type called a tjalk. *Nooit Volmaakt* means 'never perfect' in Dutch, but I don't agree, she makes a perfect home for us. She has a cosy cabin in the stern with a wood-burning stove and Obi's favourite place is curled up on the little red armchair in front of it. I prefer Mum's bunk, hidden behind patchwork curtains right under the stern. From there I can look out of the port-light to keep watch on the gangplank when we are in harbour. You never know who might try to sneak on board.

There are lots of special words to describe boats and luckily Obi and I are quick learners. We make food in the galley, and Jon taught Obi and me to swim in the mini bathtub in the heads. We built Jon his own cabin in the fo'c'sle, I helped to spread the varnish on the wooden bunk and Obi tested all the lockers. All three of us can hide in there if Mum has adult visitors, as the entrance is human kitten size and hidden behind the mast tabernacle. The mast is the big tree that we like to climb, up on the deck which is like a back yard on boats. It has lots of exciting things to play with, although Mum does get grumpy when we tangle up the lines.

Becoming barge cats did take a little getting used to. Mum explained that she couldn't cut a cat flap in the doors because they led from the stern deck where you steer the boat and sometimes waves wash over there. The first few nights I had to knead Mum on the chest to wake her up so we could go outside in our usual way, to hunt for mice and patrol our yard. She soon learned to put us out before she went to sleep, but then we had a week of rain and, however loudly I yowled outside the port light above her bed, it took ages for her to let us back in. Well I don't appreciate getting soaking wet, so Obi investigated and found a handy port light in the deck hatch above Jon's bunk that swung open when you pushed it. Jon squealed like a mouse the first time Obi jumped down and landed right on his feet! I still have to wake him up to help me if I am stuck inside and want to get out, but Obi is as agile as a square-rigger sailor. He can leap up the yard above the bunk to the hatch the port light is set in, dangle from the hatch with one paw while he hooks the port light open with the other, then hoist himself up and through in the twitch of a tail. He puzzled Mum for weeks by appearing out on deck after she had shut us inside, until Jon let her in on the secret.

It didn't take us long to get our sea legs, although I must admit I had a little *mal de mer* the first time we took the barge out of the river and out across the bar. Even snuggled under Mum's duvet my tummy was riding up and down with the barge and I couldn't bear to move until we were back in the river. Obi felt even worse, I think he was a little scared, as he hid under the floorboards in the very bows of the boat and refused to come out until we were safely anchored. He did make a useful discovery, that when you squeeze under the boards you can wriggle out of the silly padded coats Mum used to put us in whenever we left the harbour. There was no way I was going to be seen wearing one of those!

My favourite spot when we are sailing is on the cabin top, on the leeward side of the chimney. I can keep a good look out from there and give a friendly hint to whichever human is on the helm, if they are going off course or another boat is coming. When we are on the river, I can watch things on the bank, and all the landlubber shore cats can see me, which is very satisfying. You have to keep a sharp eye on the water too. One time we were anchored in the next river, near our favourite watering hole at Pin Mill, and I woke up in the night because I heard a strange snuffling sound outside. Well I immediately alerted Obi and Jon and we did a patrol. There was nothing on deck, only a strong fishy smell, and Obi was just suggesting I dreamt it when Jon hissed and pointed to the dinghy trailing off our stern, there was a big fat seal asleep inside! Jon wouldn't let us chase him off and we told Mum about it in the morning, but he had gone. He must have been grateful for the rest, as he left half an oily fish, which made a good breakfast. Ever since then I have taken to jumping into the dinghy when we are sailing along, in case he decides to come back. I've heard that seals are very good fishermen.

It's very important to keep a good watch on a barge and humans aren't very good at this, luckily, they have me and Obi to take care of things. There are a lot of water rats living around the barge harbour, and they often try to sneak aboard at night. Even when Mum remembers to hoist up the gangplank, they shimmy along the mooring lines and we have to chase them off. Mostly the humans sleep through our night watches, but one time a particularly large and vicious old rat was giving us the run around the foredeck. We called out for help from Loony, the big lurcher dog who keeps watch on the Thames barge alongside. He came aboard willingly enough, but like most dogs he's not the brightest star in the sky and started running after me, running to catch up with Obi, still chasing the rat. We yelled at Loony to turn around and catch the rat from the front, but he didn't get it, so we all ran around and round the big windlass until Jon came out to help. The rat leapt overboard, and Jon took Loony back home, but he kept grumbling about being woken up by the noise, which I thought was very ungrateful. After all, we usually save him the best specimens from our hunting trips ashore. In fact, Obi sometimes delivers especially fine voles through the port light onto his bunk, a regular home delivery service.

A barge makes a fine home, but to me she truly comes alive when we go sailing. She does have a big old truck engine, which Jon calls the iron horse, I'm not sure why because it sounds more like a growling dog. When we sail though she ripples and raps like a scat singer and rocks and rolls like a dancer. She has a big brown sail with a gaff curved like an arched cat's back. She has a flat bottom, so she sits happily in the mud at low tide. To keep her balance when she's underway she has heavy oak lee-boards that we winch up and down on the leeward side as we tack. You have to stay out of the way of the winch handle when you lower the board down, if you let the brake go too soon it spins like Obi chasing his tail and nearly broke Mum's hand once. Now I keep a careful distance and warn Mum to do the same.

Mum says the previous skipper of our barge used to race her in the Nordenzee (North Sea) with a crew of hefty Dutch sailors, but we like the way she sails steady and comfortably in all but the choppiest seas. Mum, Jon, and I all love to sit in the curve of the sail just inside the big wooden boom as she runs along, but Obi prefers the cockpit or the saloon bunks when the hatch boards are open. He's not a natural old salt like me and gets excited as soon as he spies land. When we draw closer to harbour, he runs to the end of the bowsprit as we approach the dock and leaps off as soon as we are a couple of yards away. Me, I like to supervise the crew stowing the sails and coiling the ropes, until everything's ship-shape. Then I sit on the big oak tiller, above the carving of a flying goose, and wait for Mum and the crew to head to the pub. I always follow them up the lane and across the track to the Last Anchor and sit outside while they drink their beer, sharing my salty adventures with some of the young kittens from the town. Yes, it's a good life being a barge cat.

Bio: Jane was born with salt in her veins, raised messing about in boats and has owned several. Currently she lives aboard the sailing yacht SV *Chantey* with her husband Ivan (Greybeard), anchored in El Salvador (Pacific side) getting ready to sail south and through the Panama Canal, to be nearer to their three sons and six grandchildren in England. A writer, educator and activist, Jane loves sewing, playing the accordion and getting involved in local communities as she voyages.

www.svchantey.com
www.reshapers.org
ww.welearnwechange.org.uk
www.survivorsvoices.org

Pet Bio: Listy was rescued from under a garden shed and adopted by Jane and her son Jon as a one-week-old kitten. A natural sea cat, he enjoyed voyaging the East coast of England on the Dutch sailing barge that became their home.

Listy the Barge Cat (Jane Chevoux)

The Night of the Big Tip: Tales from Cruising the ICW (Intracoastal Waterway)
by Dana Sims

No one asked me for my opinion about sailing. No one asked me if I wanted to live on a boat. No one told me that I was going to have to deal with my humans and a stupid dog, 24 hours a day for four months straight. And yet, that's exactly what happened.

It was a freezing day in January when I was shoved into my crate (despite my best efforts by claw and fang) and deposited unceremoniously onto the sole of our first sailboat. I must admit, I got some joy from knowing it was a hard winter for my furless humans as they figured out how to stay warm only inches from the icy water around us. But I didn't complain too much. Nothing was all that different from being a land cat.

As the weather warmed, I started being allowed to venture out on to the decks.

And, oh my! There were flying things that squawked. Jumping things that splashed. And, the smells! Best of all, there was freedom!

I promptly left the boat.

I didn't even have to bribe the stupid dog for her silence. Over and over, the humans would discover my absence and return me to the boat. Rinse, and repeat. You know how it goes.

One day, the humans were particularly distracted. So, I explored a little further than usual. I slinked along the dock real quiet, checking out this really interesting smelling fishing boat.

And then, plop!

Next thing I knew, I found myself bobbing in the near freezing water alongside the previously mentioned fishing boat. My life flashed before my eyes. The kibble. The nip. The day the stupid dog got stuck in the bathtub! Cozy blankets. Warm pets from the humans.

Oh, the felinity!

Just as I thought all was lost, a stranger scooped me out of the ice water. Oh, how I hugged that human! He returned me dripping wet to my humans.

As I spent hours cleaning off the disgusting flavored water, I vowed never again to leave the boat.

Not long after that, the humans began staying home all the time. No longer did I enjoy the daily breaks from their constant jabbering and demands to pet me. They had taken what they called a 'sea-battical'.

Day after day, my nap schedule was disrupted because they needed to sit where I was sleeping. Or, they needed to lift the floorboard I'd staked out for a nap. And, of course, they kept putting away the soft things I found to snuggle into.

It was exhausting!

Then one afternoon, a loud rumble began below the boat. The floor began to vibrate. My feet slid a bit one way, then the other.

I panicked!

My human said the vomit I left on the floor for them was because I got seasick. I stand behind my story that I was just disgusted with this whole endeavor. Many hours later, the rumble went silent and floors stopped moving.

I could hear the humans quiet-yelling at each other – something about throwing a line and getting too close to the dock and "Stop yelling, the people at the docks can hear you!"

I thought for certain that would be the end. Yet, day after day, it started again as we made it down the Intracoastal Waterway.

Eventually, I became accustomed – mostly – to this whole thing they called 'sailing'. I found the perfect spot in the companionway to lay throughout the day. It was perfect because I could put my paws on either side and stay balanced if the boat leaned too far over to one side or the other. Adding to the perfection was that the humans had to step over me every time they wanted to go in and out of the boat.

I'll admit it. There was a small part of me that hoped they might fall down the stairs. I mean, you know. Just a little fall. A bit of a reminder that I was the boss – even though no one asked me for my opinion about sailing. No one asked me if I wanted to live on a boat. No one told me that I was going to have to deal with my humans and that stupid dog for 24 hours a day for four months straight.

I continued to try to escape periodically. We'd arrive into port. The humans would become lax. I'd make for land. Sadly, one or the other of the humans always found me and deposited me right back onto the boat.

I will say though, I grew a little respect for the stupid dog. She never made a sound whenever I made a run for it. She minds her own business, if you know what I mean.

This continued on for weeks.

Although I'd never admit this to the humans – it began to grow on me. The consistency of the days. The food was unremarkable. But, the new smells each day! Different kinds of flying things and splashing things to watch. The humans stopped quiet-yelling at each other as much as they got a hang of 'docking'. And, it got to the point that it wasn't really worth trying to escape anymore.

Dare I say, I began to relish the life of a pirate kitty?

And, then it happened. The night of the Big Tip.

It started off as any other night.

The humans cooked things on the grill that they wouldn't share. They had some drinks and went to bed. Every few hours one or the other human would wake up to check the 'glowy box' to see where we were. They were obsessed with something they called 'dragging'.

It was out of the ordinary when I started hearing some loud whispering in their room. And, then suddenly… the boat tipped over!

Their things began to slide. Loud noises of things falling on the floor could be heard throughout the boat. One of the humans, nearly naked as the day she was born, raced up the stairs to look out into the pitch black to see why the boat was tipping over.

I had to chuckle a little. Humans have no night vision, so she couldn't see anything. No one asked me, of course. But, if they had, I could have told them that the water around us was falling.

The other human dressed quicker than usual, while the first human demanded, "Call Towboat US to find out if we are in imminent danger!"

And, so he did. I mean, he never actually asked that question, but he did tell her that someone was on their way out to make sure we were ok. Unsatisfied with that answer, the first human decided we were to abandon ship. Quickly, she began shoving me into this yellow 'life jacket'.

I did my best to resist. For one, I'm not the kind of cat that debases himself by wearing clothes. For another, I've been in the water before. It's cold. And, I don't like it.

So, after she got my jacket on and turned her attention to hauling the stupid dog's jacket on – I took my jacket off. Yet again, I wasn't asked for my opinion. But this time, I was taking a stand. I would not be pushed around and forced into the water. Or, that terrible jacket!

You would not be surprised to know that she had some choice words about my decision.

Things continued to slide around us. The boat continued to tip further and further over.

Frustrated with my jacket decision, the human decided to put my crate together to try to force me into that instead. Silly human! With the boat continuing to tip over, a few of the clips for the crate slid down the floor and dropped right into the hole they call the bilge.

Not to be put off, she shoved me into the crate anyway. Again, despite my best efforts (of both claw and fang) I found myself locked into the crate.

Next, she set off back up to the top of the boat to release the mini-boat that she meant to be our rescue.

That, my friends, did not turn out well.

You see, our boat had tipped so far over at this point that none of us (especially me in the stupid crate) could have gotten into the mini-boat. Plus, as she'd later found out, there was only about two or three feet of water below us anyway. We could have all just walked to shore if she was so determined to escape.

Anywaaaay...

The human from Towboat US eventually arrived. After assuring my humans that they were not in imminent danger, he spent the next few hours making conversation as the boat continued to tip. He explained tides to them.

From my crate, my heart grew with joy as the humans became embarrassed with their mistake. You see, in Florida there are six-foot tides. This is quite different from the two-foot tides of the Chesapeake that they'd grown so accustomed to.

Between their charts not being completely accurate and their calculation of where they were in the tide when they anchored – we ended up with much less than the five feet of water we needed to stay afloat.

As the sun began to rise, so did the water. The Towboat US human pulled us to the safety of deeper water and helped us anchor again. Exhausted, my humans trudged down the stairs half eaten by mosquitos and released me from my jail. We all climbed back into bed to snuggle (even the stupid dog) – at least until fishing boats decided that it was their job to rock our boat. Little did they know – their wakes were nothing compared to our night of The Big Tip.

Pet Bio: Some assume my name is short for Hemingway, but I was named after a hemi engine for my superior purring skills. In my 13 years I've lived in Florida, Virginia, Washington DC, and now Maryland with my humans and a stupid dog. We moved aboard our boat in 2018 with plans to head down the ICW as short-term cruisers.

The stupid dog is in charge of our social media and keeps a running commentary on our lives aboard SV *Sea Paws*. Meanwhile, I spend my days sleeping on various cushions, laying in the sun, and eating. I enjoy stealing meat from the human's dinner plates, escaping from the boat, and ignoring the dog.

Bio: A professional - turned sailor. After 10 years in grad school to receive her doctorate, Dana spent another 10 years working as a Federal employee. As a published author and speaker, she co-founded Fedability, aimed at helping government employees have successful, fulfilling careers.

Then the sailing bug bit her.

Dana and her boyfriend dreamed of the freedom of life in the blue waters of the Caribbean. After four years of planning, downsizing, saving, and taking sailing classes, they bought their first sailboat. Soon after, they took a short sabbatical from their government jobs to sail the Intracoastal Waterway. Many encouraged them to document their experiences. It was then that the Willow Sea Paws Facebook page was created to detail their (mis)adventures from the eyes of their pets.

Less than a year after returning to their 'real' jobs from sabbatical, they could no longer resist the call of the water and resigned from their Federal positions. Both turned in their titles of Doctor for Skipper and First-Mate. To their friends and fans, they are better known as Willow's Sheeple. Hemi, their cat, doesn't get much of a voice in their travels. But if he did, there would be more where this story came from.

https://www.facebook.com/WillowSeaPaws/

Hemi (Dana Sims)

Sailing with Pancakes
by Lauren Demos

Sailing with cats. It should be easy, right?

That's how Hemingway (polydactyl*) cats came to the US, and sailing was an accepted form of travel for cats for many years. Cats were shipboard creatures on many sailing vessels, since they kept the rodents at bay, and thus the communicable diseases like tularaemia and bubonic plague that the rodents carried.

But today, it's more of a rarity.

I'm a feline-only veterinarian. I'm new to sailing myself. I never thought I'd be out sailing, let alone that I'd find a feline companion to be a fellow sailor.

Earlier this year I bought a sailboat. I had already been taking my cat, Pancake, (and yup, she resembles one) paddle boarding with me. I wanted to show people that cats are great adventure companions – superior to dogs, in many ways. Smaller, they travel more easily, eat less (so less supplies to carry), and occupy less of a sleeping footprint (helpful on a paddle board or small sailboat). I figured I may have met the perfect first mate. So, when she tolerated a PFD and would go for neighborhood walks on a harness, I figured sailing was in both our futures. We started by spending a night or a day at the dock, on the boat. It went well. The night herons were a bonus and highly intriguing to Pancake – who knew birds that big existed? The dock staff dusting cobwebs in the morning were also intriguing but greeted with much less enthusiasm.

Eventually, we decided to see how an actual day sail would be with a cat. Humored by my good friend Steve – and on an 18-foot sailboat none-the-less, the most excitement came when the sails were dropped through the front hatch: "Really? I was sleeping here, guys!"

This summer, I upgraded to my own Contessa 26. Legendary as a boat. And legendary for its feline passengers as well (Tanya Aebi and Tarzoon quickly come to mind). Why couldn't Pancake and I do the same?

After spending most of the summer sailing my new boat from Maine to Michigan (with more help from Steve and others, and more humoring) my boat was finally in home-waters and ready to be 'Pancake-tested'.

The marina occupants found this idea... hilarious? Amazing? Dubious? I had a mixed bag of reactions, but everyone was smiling, no matter their assessment. "A cat on a sailboat?" they asked. They were incredulous.

We did two nights at anchor on our first weekend, with a 30-mile open water crossing in-between. If anything, the struggle for Pancake was finding the best sunny spot through the portlights – tough day. The next day involved some tame sailing, and some scenic gazing through the lifelines was in order.

Sailing with cats is an adventure.

Now, don't get me wrong, it's not all easy as (Pan)cakes.

At 3 am, Pancake had found out the location of the sandwich fixings and managed to wrangle those out for a bite.

At 4 am, Pancake decided that the quarter berth was the only spot suitable for sleeping, who cares that a grown human can barely find the room to stretch out there.

At 5 am, Pancake learned that by standing on said human, she could now see out the portlights.

Once safely back to the marina, the situation quickly deteriorated. Everyone now wanted to stop and talk about their cats, and how they could get them out onto their boats: sailing or motor vessels. It's tough to eat dinner that way, with a steady stream of people wanting to stop and pat the cat but gratifying to see the engagement. And it's exactly the reason I want to do this: cats have long had the short end of the stick. And it's time for that to change.

So how does it start?

Find the right cat. Some cats are cats, and some cats are basically dogs. Pick a dog cat to start. Gregarious. Curious. It helps if they are slightly cute or have a distinguishing feature like my one-eyed cat named Dude – everyone loves Dude.

Train them to have a harness, but find ways to make it enjoyable with treats, and positive reinforcements. Use a harness that is meant for dogs – the 'H' style harnesses for cats don't fit well, I would imagine are uncomfortable, and don't secure well. Keep the harness on at all times when the boat is open to the environment, so you have a grab point (think man overboard with a boat hook).

Sailing with Pancakes is a joy. Every time I go out, I look forward to those cats' paws: both outside the boat, as we all do, but I love having the cat's paws inside, as well.

*A polydactyl cat is a cat with a congenital physical anomaly that causes the cat to be born with more than the usual number of toes on one or more of its paws. They became known as Hemingway cats after Ernest Hemmingway was given a white, six-toed cat called Snowball by a visiting sea captain.

Bio: Lauren Demos BGS BSc (Vet Biol) BVMS Hons (Vet Virology), Past President, American Association of Feline Practitioners; Board of Directors, Veterinary Information Network VIN Associate Editor; Feline Internal Medicine. Lauren sails a Contessa 26.

Pancake (Lauren Demos)

Flying Kittens
by Jackie Parry

I am quite convinced they sat on their haunches, pulled on thick-soled heavy boots (black I think), and laced them up grinning like, well yes, Cheshire Cats!

That's what it sounded like anyway.

Clomp, Gallop, Clomp, Gallop ... silence ... (my shoulders tense) ... *bang! ... clompety clompety clomp.*

"Just what on earth are they doing?"

"Erm, running I guess."

Noel wasn't happy, he doesn't like cats at the best of times. Only because they make him sneeze. Have you ever noticed that cats gravitate to people who don't want them near?

It all started when we dragged anchor. Noel was ashore buying a part for the boat. The wind gusted to about 20 knots and we slowly moved. In the tightly packed bay (with poor holding), in the Canary Islands it wasn't long before we were too close to another boat.

"Andy," I sung out, "would you mind if I just tied up alongside you and move when Noel comes back? I'll keep the engine on for a bit in case I cause you to drag too."

Andy was happy, and we efficiently secured the boats alongside, the wind eased, and we sat comfortably together.

We stayed this way for three days. Andy was a nice quiet guy, and content enough to have us as neighbours. The boats swung peacefully, except... those kittens.

He was such a likeable character, Andy. The cruisers at anchor arranged pot-lucks that were easy and sociable, but I sensed a tragedy was still raw on his nerves – he was happy to socialise but not maintain long term contact with emails. As a single-hander he had sought company of the furry kind, rescuing two kittens. They were gorgeous. They were also two little bundles of mischievous energy.

Now we were rafted up, and much to those fluff-balls' delight their playground doubled in size! Now there were two nice sizeable decks to gallop around, new lines to leap on, a new windlass to hide behind, and a new tall mast to try to climb!

I loved it as much as they did. I love all animals, including cats, much to Noel's dismay.

But have you ever heard cats gallop across your deck, flat out, bundling along, scrapping, playing, and generally causing mayhem?

"How can something so soft and small make so much noise!" This was Noel's favourite saying for the next three days, as well as, "AND AT NIGHT!"

It made me smile. I could hear the joy in their paw-steps.

The time came to separate the boats, the kittens turned this into a game. As we loosened the lines the boats drifted a few inches apart, the kittens appeared and leapt onto our boat.

"Oh no you don't you little rascals, back you go." I scooped them up and gently plopped them down on Andy's boat. They ran off and the boats separated a little more. The kittens didn't falter, and they leapt back on board!

I quickly grabbed them and threw them across the gap of about two feet, back to Andy.

Unperturbed, and sensing a great game, they galloped in a sweeping arc and leapt across once again, onto our boat.

"For the love of cats!" By this time, I was laughing, and Noel wasn't.

"Just throw them back," Andy called.

The distance was now several feet, I didn't relish convincing them to take a dinghy ride with me later to transport them home that way. I snatched them up and threw them back one at a time. I know cats are good on their feet and I knew these two were extra agile.

Flying cats through the air! Off they went. I am sure I heard a squeal of delight.

I'd never hurt another living thing in my life, so please be rest assured I would not have done this had I not been certain they'd be fine.

As the fur-balls left my hands for the air, legs akimbo as if taking lessons from Australia's gliding possums, Noel gunned the engine. With lines clear we put as much distance as possible between the two boats.

The kittens watched us leave, tugging at my heart. I'd enjoy a good night's sleep, but they had purred their way deep into my soul. Although young and silly, they stayed on Andy's boat, their home. I miss those little monsters and their pounding paws – how can something so small make a noise so big!

Bio: Jackie Parry has circumnavigated the globe one and a half times. She is a maritime teacher, author of four books, and co-editor of SisterShip Magazine. Jackie lives in rural NSW with her husband Noel and four horses, Ned, Charlie, Dom, and Joe.

http://www.noelandjackiesjourneys.com
https://jackieparry.com
https://www.amazon.com/Jackie-Parry/e/B00OT9CWV8
www.sistershipmagazine.com

How I Crossed the Atlantic Aboard a Sailing Ship with my People by Daria Blackwell

Fond Farewells

"Goodbye, my friends. Goodbye, Chipmunks, I'll miss playing with you most, Chip and Dale," said Onyx as she prepared to set off on a great adventure. She was all packed and was now just visiting the neighbors to say her farewells.

"But Onyx, how will we know you are alright? Will you write to us or send us word? Will you come back for a visit?" asked Chip. "No, I'm afraid I won't be coming back. We're going to live in Ireland! They speak the same language there my People said, just with a different accent. I hope I can understand. I'll try to get word back through the People," explained Onyx.

"Farewell, Mr. and Mrs. Squirrely. We won't be playing tag across the yard anymore," said Onyx. "Oh, Onyx, do you really have to go?" said Mrs. Squirrely, "It's really scary to think about crossing oceans on a boat."

"Don't worry, Mrs. Squirrely, I've been sailing since I was a baby. I know what I'm doing." *At least I think so*, thought Onyx

"Bye, stupid Dog, who never remembers how long his chain is. I'll really miss taunting you every day," said Onyx to the Malamut tied to the tree next door. She always had so much fun walking right up to where the chain stopped him. He would come lunging at her, only to almost strangle himself on the chain when it ran out. *He would never learn*, thought Onyx as she smiled to herself. He thought of her as Karate Kitty because she whacked him a couple of times when he tried to get to know her at first. Just then he barked like mad and lunged to the end of his chain. Onyx calmly got up and walked away. She'll miss her games with him.

"Good bye, dear Deer. I won't be watching you eating out of the bird feeder anymore. I hope the new people fill it with your favourite seeds in the winter," said Onyx.

"Good bye, wild Turkey, I won't be watching you gobble gobble anymore," said Onyx as the turkey scrambled out of the bushes.

"Good bye, Siamese twins next door and good riddance. I won't have to protect my territory and throttle you anymore," said Onyx cheerfully. *Those Siamese cats thought they owned the world. But I showed them who is boss. I whacked them but good. They deserved it.*

"Good-bye, red Robin. I loved watching you come and go from your house under the eaves, especially when I could hear your babies peeping inside. Oh, if only one had fallen out. I would have been right there to catch him for you," said Onyx as she trembled just thinking about the possibility.

"Good bye, Rocky Raccoon, you won't be sneaking up on me at night anymore," said Onyx, "Good luck foraging."

"Good bye, Groundhog, I won't be waiting endlessly at the end of your smelly tunnels for you to show yourself anymore."

"Good bye, beautiful Flutterby, I'll miss chasing you and jumping as high as I can to fly with you."

And so, her good byes were coming to an end. "Good bye my garden, I'll miss sniffing your sweet flowers and sleeping in your shade. Good bye house, I'll miss finding a different nook and cranny to sleep in every day."

And with her last good bye, and a tear in her eye, Onyx climbed into the car with her people. *Let the adventures begin*, she thought.

I am Onyx, the Cruising Kitty. I am going to see the world. But first I'll have to take a nap.

All Aboard

They drove to the place where their floating home was. Onyx hated the car. It kept moving this way and that. How was anybody to sleep? When they finally arrived at the boat, she jumped on board and quickly settled herself into a nook to nap.

The next thing she knew, they were moving. Her people had loaded the boat up with all kinds of stuff. It was so full she didn't know where to move. How would she find her food bowl in all this? *I'll have to scoot through everything to check it out. Just to be sure they haven't forgotten any of my stuff. I packed so carefully, too,* she thought.

Onyx climbed over things and under things. They sure did bring a lot of stuff. *How long was this trip going to be?* she wondered. Just as she was ready to give up, she found her bowls, right where she'd left them, and they were full. *Yippee!* thought Onyx. Everything was just where she had left it. Food, shrimp juice, and poopatorium. Now she was in business. Now she was ready to set out to sea.

She climbed into her sea berth snug under the foulies and promptly started to snore.

Onyx, the Cruising Kitty was going to see the world. But first, of course, she'd have to take a nap.

Are We There Yet?

For days on end, they sailed, and sailed, and sailed some more. Onyx was very careful and never came on deck when things weren't settled. One morning, the sun was shining, and the sea was calm. Onyx heard chatter all around the boat. She gingerly ventured out on deck and there she saw something jumping out of the water and swimming alongside really, really fast.

"What was that?" asked Onyx as she meowed the question to her crew on deck.

"Oh, Onyx, those are dolphins. You've never seen them before. They've come to visit and see how we live," said her crew. "They live in the water and eat fish and shrimp, just like you do, but they catch them all by themselves."

Wow, fresh shrimp? thought Onyx, *Maybe I should jump in and swim with them.* But just then a big wave lifted the stern of the boat and two dolphins swimming in the wave were looking down at them.

"Don't jump," cried Onyx as the wave glided below their keel and the dolphins swam off.

"And look Onyx, a flying fish landed on the deck overnight, you're going to have sushi for breakfast."

"Oh good, I was getting hungry and wondering when you'd fix me something," Onyx purred.

After breakfast, Onyx went back on deck. Her crew said, "Onyx, look there are whales swimming over to us. They're huge fin whales, bigger than our boat."

"Huge? Whales? Bigger than our boat?" Onyx took one look just as the whale came up for air and blew through its blowhole. "Ugh, it smells like fish. Lots of fish," she puckered up her nose as she ran below to hide.

She snuggled up with the other crew member who was sleeping in the warm bunk. That was her job after all, to keep company with the crewmember who was off watch and share her warmth.

Soon she fell asleep and another day had passed.

"Land ho," someone was shouting, "Land ho."

Onyx and her friend woke up in a hurry and rushed out on deck wondering what all the fuss was about.

"Look Onyx, the mountains there, and the island next to them. That's home Onyx. We've sailed across the ocean. We're on the other side of the Atlantic. We're home."

Onyx sniffed the air. It smelled clean and fresh and full of scents that hadn't been there on the water. The sun was streaming through the clouds, painting the land with vivid colors. As they got closer, Onyx could see how green it was. It was very, very green.

So, this home, thought Onyx. *Green hills coming down to a bright blue sea. It's pretty here. And they must have lots of fish and shrimp. I wonder if I'll make friends here?*

Onyx, the Cruising Kitty was going to see the world. But first, of course, she'd have to take a nap.

Bio: Daria Blackwell is Rear Commodore of the Ocean Cruising Club and also the PR Officer and web editor. She is co-author of Happy Hooking the Art of Anchoring and Cruising the Wild Atlantic Way of Ireland. She has also written for many sailing publications on both sides of the Atlantic and has released a nautical murder mystery The Naked Truth. Daria and her husband Alex sail their Bowman 57 ketch in European waters these days and live in Ireland otherwise.

https://aleriasadventures.blogspot.com/

Pet Bio: Onyx, the black magic cat, set off on an adventure aboard a 57-foot boat with her two favorite people. She was a great sailor, having started sailing at the age of 6 weeks. She'd been preparing for this her whole life. She had all her vaccinations, her passport, and a microchip. She had great sea legs but didn't like to venture off the boat, not even when docked at a marina. She did, however, keep a close eye on all the goings on. She loved to help by pulling ropes. She also knew all the best places to nap when the boat was at anchor and the ones that were better underway. Onyx crossed the Atlantic with her people three times all told. She spent a year aboard for a Caribbean circuit then ensconced herself in her new home in Ireland to write a book about her adventures. It's called, Onyx the Cruising Kitty. She had continued to cruise with her pals around the European side of the Atlantic on exciting adventures for years. Sadly, Onyx passed away from cancer and was buried under a dolmen with a view of the sea and a bird feeder overhead. Onyx, the Cruising Kitty had seen a lot of the world. Now she's taking a long nap.

Onyx (Daria Blackwell)

All Paws on Deck:
The True Story of One Cat's Transition from Landlubber to Nauti-cat
by Sandra Tretick

Meow! I'm Nukaat and this is my story. I'm not so good with computers. Walking across the keyboard is one thing, but typing is hard work. I'm all paws. So, I've dictated this to one of my assistants.

I don't like to talk much about my early years in the before times. I was always hungry then. Eventually my belly got the better of me. Some people caught me and fed me. Then one day, these other people came to meet me. I pretty much ignored them, but they stuck me in a box anyway and took me away.

They took me to their home. It didn't take long to settle in. This was a time of lounging in boxes and playing in paper bags. I even had my own kitty door. Life was good, and my assistants were quite handy at things like feeding me, petting me, and wrestling.

But things always change. One day I was put back in my box and we drove to another new place. When I finally got to roam on my own, I found a really cool pond. There were fish and birds, and bunnies and mice, and all sorts of things to chase. I left the deer alone. They were bigger than me. I liked to snooze there. It was cool among the trees. Life was looking up.

Just as my fur coat started to thicken up for winter things changed again. First, my assistants took me to a doctor a couple of times. He seemed pretty nice until he gave me a bunch of pokes and pills and stuck a computer chip inside me. Ouch, that stings! I've heard it will help identify me if I ever get lost. I don't know what all the fuss is about. I always come home for dinner.

One of my assistants did a lot of running around, apparently on my behalf. She said she had to visit the Canadian veterinarian in Victoria and then some place called the Philippines Consulate in Vancouver.

Not long after that, they put me back in the box and we went to another new place called an airport where there were lots of people standing around. I didn't know what was going on. My eyes were big, taking it all in. My assistant handed me off to a strange man in a vest and he carted me away. I didn't like it.

The next thing I knew I was put inside a small room with a bunch of bags. And then this awful loud noise started and the whole room started to shake. It seemed like forever. It's hard to tell time in the dark, but I'm pretty sure I missed out on breakfast.

Finally, the shaking stopped and another man carried me outside. The sun was just coming up and it was hot already. Like an oven. Suddenly I saw my assistant. She made all sorts of friendly noises, so I felt a little better. There were lots of other people around and I still had to be on my toes.

She put my box onto a cart and wheeled me over to a counter. The man there wore a badge that said Philippines Quarantine. He took some papers and handed her some others and then we went outside. There were all sorts of new smells. I saw my other assistant, so I figured we'd be home soon.

Boy was I wrong. We got into a car and drove for a long time. At least it was cool inside. They made me stay in the box but by now I was so tired I didn't care anymore. I curled up and had a nap. When I woke up, they carried my box alongside this enormous pond with big things floating in it. And then we climbed up onto one of them and went inside. My assistants called it a boat.

That was lots of human years ago, back when I was three or four. Now I'm nine. Or maybe ten. Far too many years to count on all my paws, anyway.

Those early days on the boat were fun, even if my assistants didn't let me go outside right away. At least there were lots of nooks and crannies to explore. I especially liked poking my nose into the bilge thingies under the floor!

This nautical life isn't too bad most of the time. These days, I stare at my assistants each morning until they finally wake up and feed me. Breakfast hasn't changed too much from my old home to this floaty one, so that's a relief.

After breakfast it's 'furminating' time! That's my favourite part of the day (after feeding time, and play time, and sleepy time). The heat can be a bit uncomfortable when you're sporting a luxurious fur coat like mine. There really aren't any seasons, just hot and wet, or hot and dry. Winters in Canada gave me a good reason to grow my coat even thicker and then shed it everywhere in spring. (You'd think my coat would thin out a little here, but it just keeps on growing and growing and shedding and shedding. It gets everywhere. That's my revenge.)

After 'furminating', I get to have some yummy brown goupy stuff that I'm told will help prevent hair balls. One time my assistant slipped on one in the dark. That was kind of funny, but she yelled out so loudly that I made myself scarce.

During the hottest part of the day, I mostly lay low in one of my favourite sleeping spots. I have a few choice ones now, but I like to mix it up from time to time so my assistants have to look for me. One of my favourite hiding spots is under the kayak thingies on deck. It's cool there, I can watch what's going on and I'm hard to reach.

I like to sit and watch my assistants when they are making food (in case there might be something tasty for me) and when they wash the dishes. I don't know why they don't just lick them clean the way I do. It's so much simpler.

Somebody usually starts play time when I'm right in the midst of a good nap. How rude! But I generally forgive them and join right in. My favourite toy is a cable tie. Nights are the best time to play. It's fun to dash up and down the stairs and back and forth making as much noise as possible when my assistants are sleeping.

Sometimes we stay in the marina place. It took me the better part of my first year on board to get the hang of jumping from the deck to the dock and back again, but once I ventured out into the bigger world, there was no looking back.

I loved these escapades under the cover of darkness. There were tiny scurrying crabs in the cracks of the dock and small fish that splashed in the water just out of my reach. Once I was tucked safely under a dinghy on another boat, people watching. Another time I made it all the way to land and was hiding in the bushes by the pool. My assistants came looking for me with a bag of treats.

A couple of times I misjudged the distance from the boat to the dock. Each time I'd come back on board dripping wet. My second swim put an end to my nightly wanderings for a time. Once I started feeling more adventurous, it happened again. And then again. How embarrassing.

Despite my assistants' best attempts to corral me, each time I came back soaked, I'd squirm and squirt my way around the saloon, the galley and the master stateroom, jump up onto counters and get everything covered in salt water as I'd try my best to out-maneuver them. When they'd finally snag me, they'd wrap me in a towel and rub my fur with wet cloths. I'd always get a trip to the cat spa for a bath the next day.

Sometimes we go on 'an adventure.' I'm not a big fan when my boat leaves the marina place. I always skedaddle when the engine thingy starts. I dash to the big bed or I dart outside. I still haven't found a really good place to hide from all that clatter and vibration. Sometimes we'd go for just a few weeks, sometimes for several months at a time.

My boat rolls around under my paws and sometimes I get a little woozy. Walking can be extra challenging, and I've even lost my appetite a few times. My assistants keep telling me to keep my eyes on the horizon, but I don't really know what that means. I curl up in my basket and refuse to move.

The only good thing is that they give me more treats than usual. This eases their guilt for subjecting me to so much torture. I may need to work on my woebegone look a little more, though. I can't help myself. I perk right up whenever I hear the crinkle of the treat bag. I think they might be on to me.

Anyhow, at least they usually stop moving in the afternoons and shut off that loud noise and we stay put overnight. I'm much happier when we stop. I bounce back to my usual self pretty quick cos it usually means it's time for dinner. There's no sense in being mopey all the time.

When we stop for the night, they say we're 'on the hook.' When that happens, there's water on all sides and no docks to tempt me.

Evenings are the best. We'd all sit outside together, and it was usually a bit cooler than mid-day. Sometimes I'd go on an inspection around.

Sometimes I simply liked to stretch out, belly up, and let the cool breeze blow across my fur. Sometimes I'd even stay out all night on watch.

Rainy days are kind of fun too. I like to drink the water that pools on deck. It's refreshing. But I don't really like to get my paws too wet. On sunny days the deck gets extremely hot and then I don't like to walk on it either. I'm pretty good at following the shade as it moves around.

One of my favourite adventures happened one evening when we were on the hook. A flock of little birds chased a swarm of flying ants around and around the boat. It was so exciting! I wasn't sure whether I should chase the bugs or the birds, but I made a good show of dashing up and down the deck.

More recently, they took me for my first ride in the dinghy thingy. That was a bit nerve wracking even though we putt-putted slowly to a small sandy island nearby. It was also my first trip to the beach. I think my assistants thought I would really like it there, but I wasn't too sure about the whole experience. There was nowhere to hide so I tucked myself back into my beach bag until it was time to go.

Earlier this year, we left the marina place again. For the next four months we moved south from one place to another. Sometimes we'd stop for one night and move on the next morning. Sometimes we'd stop in one place for a week or two or even a month. It didn't really matter too much to me, as long as they fed me on time.

On this latest adventure, my assistants told me we left the Philippines and arrived in Malaysia. I have to say that this new marina place looks a lot like the old one. I haven't had time to explore the docks or been swimming yet, mostly because there's a monitor lizard roaming around and he's a lot bigger than me.

Bio: Sandra Tretick and her husband Chris are currently cruising in SE Asia on *MV MOKEN*, a diesel Duck trawler with sails. In her home port in Canada, she worked as a communications specialist. These days she blogs about their adventures (www.moken.ca) and does a bit of freelance writing.

Pet Bio: Nukaat was rescued from almost certain starvation by Cat's Cradle Animal Rescue in Victoria, BC, Canada before joining the crew of *MOKEN*. When he was a landlubber, he loved hanging out in paper bags, lounging about in shoe boxes or sprawling out full length and belly up on the sofa. Not much has changed since he moved on board, except now the sofa is called a settee. Nukaat and his assistants are currently cruising in SE Asia.

Nukaat (Sandra Tretick)

Walter Sam: Sailing to the Andaman Islands by Jeanne Pickers

Hi everybody!

Walter Sam reporting here. (I am the Cat-Master of a catamaran (of course) in case we haven't met).

I heard my human mum and dad, and my human sister, Des, preparing for a trip from Malaysia to the Andaman Islands, and that I was to be left behind. I must say, I got quite excited at the thought of two months of freedom with a cat sitter on a neighbouring boat in the marina; but oh no... they thought poor snookums might be lonely – poo hoo. Who asked ME if I wanted to go traipsing the world on a floating piece of glass fibre when all I'm after is 'two eyes and a tail' and forty or fifty hundred winks.

Well anyway, it turned out to be quite an adventure... some of which was pretty cool... and others of which were... hmmm...

Once those engines started, I was off into my hidey-hole, thinking... NOT AGAIN! The journey started out, as usual, with all that can go wrong happening, and the boss ranting at an autopilot that wouldn't work. That didn't faze me much. But when the fridge and deepfreeze went on the blink, I certainly pricked up my ears. WHAT ABOUT MY 'TWO EYES AND A TAIL'? I ask you. Now there was a problem.

We had to stop off in Thailand to call in the experts. I bit my claws waiting for the compressor to be tested, only to find that was ok. Finally, when all four paws were chewed to the bone, a final draining of the gas and re-gassing seemed to do the trick. Whew! Problem solved, and we could head off.

This was to be Des' first ocean crossing although it was old hat to me. She was a bit nervous initially and wished that mild expletives could be confined to catastrophes (if you would excuse the pun) rather than everyday minor annoyances which my parents are apt to blurt out. I had to agree.

I got into the swing of things as it were, pretty early in the trip. It's still a mystery to me, this family of mine. They coax and cajole me out of my cubby hole whispering niceties about how wonderful it is outside and when I finally pluck up the courage to venture out and see for myself, they go crazy and want to tie me down! I mean, swinging from the boom under full sail in the middle of the night is a wonderful way to exercise and keep cool. But they seemed to go into panic mode and out comes the harness and I am strapped to the wheel. Anyway, a bit of sulking always gets me a treat, so I practiced that in-between trying to keep occupied inside *Katrine*. I conjured up all sorts of ways – my favourite being the 'lets-shred-a-new-roll-of-paper-towel' game which certainly gets their attention. Or, 'sharpen-my-claws-on-the-saloon-cushions' which I do with my eyes tightly shut and my ears back because I know I'm going to get a fat slap for my troubles. But despite all that, the best thing about the passage was that there was someone at my beck and call all night as well as all day. Hoo boy. I had them on their toes.

I must say, though, I was happy when we eventually arrived in Port Blair and had the whole crew coming on board at the same time. What a squash. Coast Guard, Customs, and Immigration all descending and oohing and ahhing at me and my new boat-made passport. I do sport a good photo, I must say, and they made a huge fuss of me.

Then with the rest of my family, Greg and Allan, flying in from Australia for two weeks, our added family meant more attention. We became the trilogy – Father, Son and the Holy Terror. The six of us set off fishing at last. This was going to be a whole new adventure I overheard, because we were going south and then on to the west side of the islands to new fishing grounds. That got me going – my tongue was hanging for fish by this time. It wasn't long before the line was zinging, and pandemonium reigned as everyone grabbed rods and hauled in my 'two eyes and a tail'. I was thrilled at the thought of fresh fish until it was finally pulled up on board. HOLY MOLEY! What was I to do with THAT? This giant wet slippery THING was hurled over the transom, splat onto the floor in front of me. Enormous eyes and a whale tail that thrashed and bounced at me. I was off back to my cubby hole to feign nonchalance till THAT was out of the way. Later that evening at the anchorage, curiosity got the better of me and I ventured onto the top step to watch Allan-the-gilly cleaning the monster. It SMELT like my 'two eyes and a tail' and the aroma got me very interested. In fact, a little too interested it turned out. Did someone once say, "Curiosity killed the Cat?" Well it was a close one for me this time. In my excitement to see all this fresh fish cleaned and gutted, I stepped down to have a sniff and take a swat at it to make sure... and woah over I went. But no problem. Allan was there to rescue me, and I got a bath and fluffing out of it which I played up to for the next few days, smelling like roses. I couldn't do a thing wrong after that.

Well the gang snorkelled and dived, and fished and fished, and the catches just got bigger and bigger. Best of all was when we anchored off Twin Island where I could do my own snorkelling from the top of the bimini. The water was that beautiful azure and glass-like. Looking down I could watch all those meals swimming round and round. It was like shopping in the deli of a supermarket down there. All well and good till the manta rays came through. Now that brought on a bit of excitement with the family in the water swimming around with them for hours and hours. I could have stayed there forever, but those humans are strange. Off we went overnight to look for a reef in the middle of the ocean that they had spied on their C-MAP charts. It was a bumpy sail, so I headed off to my cubby hole till it calmed down and lo and behold, the next morning dawned bright and calm. There we were surrounded by a full circle of horizon and looking down from my hiding place in the sail-bag, I could see the bottom of the ocean again! Well the mob was at it once more, and if I thought the fish were big that had been caught up until then – these were Monsters. Not only that, Greg dived down and produced bright green, flappy, hard-shelled things with spiky protrusions that everyone raved about. Not me. Crayfish are overrated, scary, and definitely inaccessible.

Oh, how I missed my little 'two-eyes-and-a-tail' from the Malaysian market – but it was novel. There we were anchored for the night in the middle of the ocean. Awesome.

There was only one other minor mishap when I climbed into the dinghy that evening to explore the smells and took a leap to try and get back onto the boat. Nearly clonked my lights out and was in a bit of a panic because no one knew that I hadn't made it and was in the drink again! But someone eventually heard my scrabbling and once again I was pampered and cooed over like a king

There was a distinct sadness once the boys had flown back to Australia, and I must say, even I felt the huge empty space that was left. But that's our cruising life, and we know that we must make the times we have together special and savour every minute of it. After a pep talk, we left for the islands to the east to chill out and relax for the last couple of days.

My family discovered a new favourite diving reef here, and I couldn't entice them out of the water at any cost. So, I made plans. One morning, I heard someone say that they were definitely going to catch a fish especially for me. It didn't take long and there it was flapping and slapping as it was brought under control. A Rainbow Runner – my favourite. I waited till all the fuss had quietened down and then just as I thought breakfast was on the way, they dived overboard and went snorkelling. Couldn't believe my whiskers. I took a snifty around and found it in the sink. A few paw slaps to make sure it was quite dead, then I dragged it out, over the tabletop and made myself comfortable on the saloon cushions to feast. Whew! That was a mammoth feed – a whole side of rainbow runner and my man-can was bursting. There I was, fat as a tick, and fast asleep dreaming about a change in diet when they returned, and all hell broke loose. Still can't figure it out. They said it was for me after all.

Talking about a change in diet.,. another bafflement. They complain and whine about bird poo on the boat. Then when I do them a favour and catch one of the wily, feathered playthings, and pandemonium breaks out. I get thwacked for my troubles and the little sh-stirrer is taken out of my mouth and revived. I wish they'd make up their minds. Not only that, when it tries to fly away and lands in the sea – twice – Des dives over in all her clothes to save it... I live in a strange, strange world.

Our last few days were spent at Havelock Seven. Sitting up in the cockpit I surveyed this special island. Huge trees flank miles of sandy white beach which encircles a clear blue bay – dugong, turtles, dolphin – you name it... and even elephants! Speaking of which... I had to have a laugh at those humans. They had been trying to teach me to pee in the toilet again. Something about stocks getting low and cat litter running out. So, the little blue dish of kitty litter was placed in the toilet for me every morning and I duly did my thing to please them and get a dried fish (small as it is) and an extra loving. The next stage is to remove the litter and I'm s'posed to do my ablutions in the toilet. I am rather a clever little 'so and so' actually. One morning I was about to do my bit, when someone shouted that there were elephants on the beach. Everyone, including me, made a dive for the cockpit to see, and the toilet training was forgotten. It wasn't till later in the day when all the ragging was going on that I realised that Mother M as we call Jeanne, had gone to relieve herself and not noticed the dish of kitty litter in the toilet. That was a laugh!

Well, all good things must come to an end sometime, I heard my humans sigh and we were soon sailing back to Malaysia. The weather was perfect for a brilliant sail and the dolphins were there to escort us all the way. I couldn't wait to get back to the marina and all the lizards and geckos and insects again. After all a change in diet is the essence of life. I'd had enough of 'two eyes and a tail' for now.

But of course, it was the most *Purrrfect* family holiday.

Miaaaw from me on *Katrine*.

Bio: We set sail from South Africa to start a new life in 2001 on a catamaran *Katrine* which we built on our farm. It has been an amazing adventure!

Pet Bio: Walter Sam was a tabby cat we rescued from a dockside in Malaysia as a tiny kitten after his mother had disappeared. He stole our hearts with his endearing character and gave us so much joy while cruising. Sadly, he was killed by a car when he wandered off onto a road after we had docked at a marina a year ago.

Walter Sam in the Andamans (Jeanne Pickers)

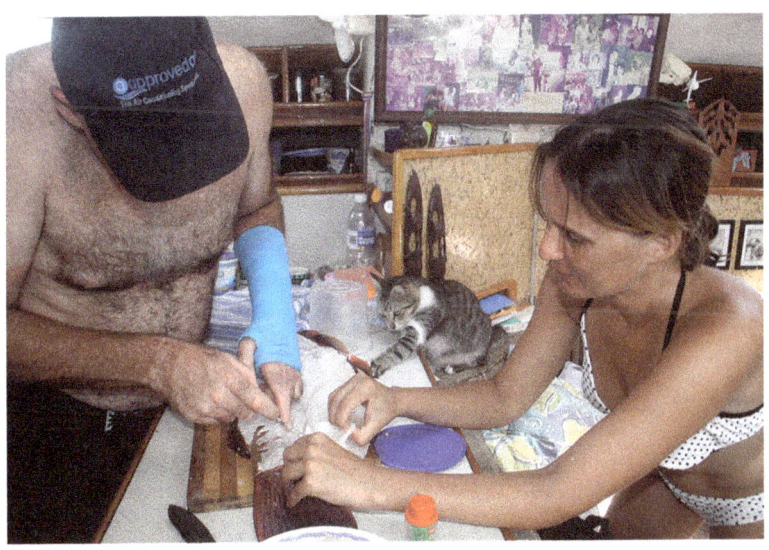

PART THREE: UNUSUAL AND 'NOT-QUITE' PETS

Roger Booby
by Justine Porter

I sometimes confirm that I've heard my husband aboard our yacht *Shima* with "Roger" instead of "yes", it's become a staple word, but little did I know that Roger would become a troublesome but delightful visitor.

In July 2016 we sailed to the wonderful island of Sweers in the southern Gulf of Carpentaria, northern Australia, to explore and play with our buddies aboard *Wildcard* and make new and lasting friendships including a brown booby bird with attitude!

Our first day on Sweers Island we were greeted by Tex and Lyn Battle and introduced to the wonderful history of this now proud fishing resort but upon returning to *Shima,* our Mumby catamaran, we were confronted by a cranky booby bird. He had traversed our decks leaving parcels of poop everywhere! Glen went on deck to shoo him away, but he obstinately stood his ground, fluffed his feathers, and squawked angrily stating that he had claimed our decks. I laughed as Glen retreated, quite defeated. This bird was not to win on my watch so I got a broom to protect myself from his sharp beak and stoic attitude, and swept him gently along the deck down the steps and onto our sugar scoop, but he just wouldn't budge at the edge, teetering holding that last piece of deck!

I figured he could do little harm down there and gave up. He looked quite proud, head held high, and carefully watched our movements!

The next morning we again went ashore to look for the remnants of Matthew Flinders visit in 1802. This island is steeped in wonderful history, but unbeknownst to us that booby-with-a-wonky-wing-feather was causing mischief back aboard!

On our return this tenacious and persistent booby had adorned our decks in poop again. Now bird poop is one thing, but booby poop is quite another, unhappy I grabbed my broom and escorted the now very defiant booby down the sugar scoop and gave him a good verbal scolding. As I turned my back he hissed at me; an acknowledgment causing us both to laugh and say, 'Roger' in unison. Our brown booby bird was duly named!

I cleaned the decks and kept looking at him, talking to him and telling him not to come on deck, gave him permission to use the sugar scoop but sternly delivered the rule book. He jumped up the first step to look at us, but I grabbed the broom and pushed him to the bottom step but no further this time, he nodded his head and looked thoughtful, did he understand? That night he tucked his head into his wonky wing and slept safely aboard *Shima*. In the morning we leaned over to see him sleeping and in unison said, 'Good morning Roger,' he jerked awake and watched our morning routine with interest.

We watched him survey the sparkling waters then take off, swooping and diving catching fish for breakfast nearby and amazingly he flew back to *Shima*. This time he looked at us and remembered his lesson, adjusted his wonky but beautiful wings, lined up our sugar scoop and landed quite precisely looking chuffed with himself. We applauded him.

For the next three weeks this became his routine – he never attempted to come onto our decks again, happy pooping resting and fishing from our sugar scoop. He certainly made a mess down there, but we were happy with our arrangement. He had attitude but seemed to respond to our chats, at times he would poke his bottom over the edge and send those big wet poops to sea.

Our time at Sweers came to an end and it was time to set sail and continue our exploration of the gulf. Roger looked perplexed as we prepped the sails, cocking his head watching intently but firmly stationed in his spot. As we motored off he teetered on the edge using his wings for balance, eventually we increased our speed and the sloshing water on the scoop forced him to take flight. He circled around us saying his goodbyes. We felt sad to go as we had become quite fond of him but the story doesn't quite end here!

The Deportation

Oh no that Roger really did have spunk, he found a new boat to poop on – he chose MV *Solomon* to be a naughty stowaway aboard. This is the main charter vessel for the resort, named after another famous explorer, and the resort owners were not impressed with his pooping ways. Roger became a menace, biting guests and stealing bait and generally tormenting them. So the skipper took Roger to the opposite side of the island and deposited him on the northern tip. The plan, however, was foiled as Roger did not like his new digs, flying all the way back and arriving at sunset just in time to deliver his trademark poops after the boat had been washed for the day.

He tried desperately to resume his spot on MV *Solomon* but the owners of Sweers were just as determined that he should go. Over a few of their famous and delicious tawny Ports a cunning scheme was devised. Roger was encouraged the next day into a large box, they quickly taped it shut and his deportation from Sweers became official. The propellers of a light plane whirled, and the pre-flight checks were made with a rather large brown box strapped into the backseat. Roger was probably wondering what all this fuss was about! The landing was smooth at Burketown about 40 nautical miles away, Roger's transition to the mainland was complete. They selected a nice area where other brown boobies soared on the winds and released him. Cheers abounded the deportation a success, Roger and his wonky wing appeared happy and unharmed!

Over the following fortnight the stories of Roger's shenanigans were shared with laughter, and maybe some sadness, at the Sweers Island bar. His squawking pecking ways, his indignant stance but most of all how that bird could poop.

At sunrise one morning a brown booby with a wonky wing flew low and slow over the resort and landed nearby on the beach. As the guests and workers came down to go fishing for the day, there he was. Roger was back. His distinctive wonky wing feather obvious and an assurance it really was him.

He looked longingly at the boats, the deportation maybe did achieve something as he certainly had learnt a lesson. He kept on the outskirts but continued to fish and love his home with only the occasional deposit on a boat as a cheeky reminder that he was still there!

Bio: Justine and Glen had their dream built in the Philippines and sailed her home in 2014, they gave up their ties to land the following year to sail and explore Australia's least known places. With a love of sea but no sailing experience they have self-taught. With close to 10,000 nm under their belts they plan to add many more.

Roger Booby (Justine Porter)

Things Wot the Cat Dragged In
by Jill Budd

Living and travelling on our narrowboat with two dogs and a cat called Daisy, it was commonplace for Daisy to return to the boat with various unfortunate creatures. Some were dead on arrival (DOA), some were rescued, and some came to live with us for a while.

The most extraordinary of which in the DOA category was, probably, a mole – it gave me quite a fright when its little pink 'hands' emerged from her mouth on a very dark night.

The prize, however, for 'greatest disruption' should go to a young rabbit.

It was a lovely sunny day and the side hatches opposite our dining area were open. We had just poured ourselves a glass of wine and started tucking in to a lovely Sunday dinner of roast beef and potatoes, with Yorkshire puddings and all the delicious trimmings. All was perfect; until Daisy jumped through the side hatch with an uninvited dinner guest – a young rabbit. Had the rabbit been dead, our dinner might have survived. She dropped it on the table, whereupon it made a miraculous recovery; kicking out with its back feet and sending wine, glasses, and roast beef crashing to the floor, before jumping off the table and careening down the remaining 16 metres of boat with Daisy and one of the dogs in hot pursuit. The other dog thought all its Christmases had come at once; beef on the floor was a far greater prize than a rabbit on the loose – he's always been a lazy dog.

Believe me when I tell you that two panicking adults within the confined width of a narrowboat are pretty ineffectual. Trying to keep the dog out of the food on the floor that was full of broken glass was our priority (although I confess that it did cross my mind that some wine might have been salvageable). Having removed him and shut him in a safe place, we set about trying to resolve 'the situation' happening down t'other end; only to find that Daisy had got bored with the whole thing and wandered off again – no doubt to find replacement prey – and the dog had cornered the rabbit, but didn't know what to do with it. The rabbit was eventually rescued and released, allowing the dog to recover his dignity, and the copious amounts of rabbit poo came out of the bedroom carpet – eventually. Beans on toast for us for dinner.

The prize for 'most intrepid' uninvited guest though – and my heart – goes to a little mouse.

Anyone who shares their living space with a cat will be quite familiar with the game known as, "Quick, catch it, it's still alive". A frequent occurrence and usually quite quickly remedied with a plastic container and a piece of cardboard. Not so for this particular little guy, who swiftly nipped into a hole in the skirting where the electrical wires disappeared behind the panelling. Mice and electrical wires are never a good combination – especially on a boat.

After two days with the only clue as to its whereabouts being Daisy's occasional fixed stare and chattering teeth, we baited humane traps. The little guy enjoyed his (I always think of him as a 'he') free meals of cheese and chocolate whilst deftly avoiding capture. By the time he considered this nutrition to be insufficient and moved into the store cupboard, we were becoming desperate and, reluctantly, put down standard mouse traps. These were treated with the same disdain as the previous ones and he continued to dine out at our expense; spending most of his evenings running around in the roof linings.

Plan 'C' was to buy chocolate flavoured blocks of rat poison, unscrew the mushroom vents and place the blocks in the ceilings above the saloon and bedroom areas.

Sitting in the saloon in the evenings we often saw his underbelly flash across the opening where we removed the vents. We also, surprisingly quickly, became accustomed to the sound of him dragging and chomping on the poison blocks, which he devoured at a surprising rate with no apparent ill effects. It would seem that he enjoyed our company as, when we retired to bed at night, he changed rooms. Within 10 minutes of our moving to the bedroom, the dragging and chomping sound would resume over our heads – additional orchestration was provided by Daisy, who would stomp around our bed gnashing her teeth at the ceiling.

After five months or so this became completely normal; although the sound effects took some explaining to guests and visitors. We kept feeding him and he kept stomping about in the ceiling, changing rooms when we did. The only thing that changed was the size of his rapidly expanding underbelly as it flashed across the openings.

By the end of the summer it was time to move the boat into the paint shed and start re-painting the roof. We prepped the roof and removed the mushroom vents from the top, ready for an early start in the morning.

Climbing onto the roof in the morning we found the little guy dead, next to the vent hole.

Tears were shed, and we gave the intrepid chap a dignified burial. I like to think he died of old age, but rather fear that the dry atmosphere in the paint shed deprived him of the condensation in the roof lining he, presumably, had been surviving on. It took quite a while for us to get used to sleeping without the sound effects in the ceiling.

Bio: I was fortunate enough to take early retirement at the age of 54; selling my craft shops and moving onto a narrowboat to cruise the British inland waterways with my husband, two dogs and two cats. After six years we shipped the narrowboat across to mainland Europe and loved it so much that we stayed; selling the narrowboat and buying an elderly Dutch Barge. We continue to cruise throughout Europe and you can follow our travels on my blog contentedsouls.com

Daisy (Jill Budd)

A Ratty Tale
by Cherylle Stone

Until he climbed on board my boat, Sir Isaac Coffin was probably loved deeply by someone.

We had spent a wonderful day wandering around picturesque Coffin Bay in South Australia having left the dinghy tied up to an ancient wharf. While we were away Sir Isaac secreted himself into the dinghy to hitch a ride out to the boat. He waited until about midnight to get aboard, waking us. We thought someone was rattling the painter and trying to nick the dinghy.

A day later I found the rags in disarray in their nook and thought the skipper was being a messy buggar. The day after that, I went to the dry foods storage and found clear evidence that we had another living creature aboard. Every packet had been breached.

I set about chucking out the spoiled food and cursing Sir Isaac as we would all have to live together on a 35-foot boat for another 10 days. We were by then underway from Coffin Bay via the scenic route to Port Lincoln and did not have a trap.

The teacher in me had a strong desire to train Sir Isaac, so each night I laid out a piece of paper towel on the sole and dressed it with dainty morsels for his delectation. He obliged as soon as the lights went out. He also mooched noisily about during the night.

Ratting around is an apt turn of phrase. It included displacing the insulation and making a tissue nest in the stove, discovered when smoke started billowing up the wall behind it.

Of course, we hoped that his need to chew would not cause too many electrical problems. In fact, we hoped his choice of chewing wire and a potential electrocution would be on something not too important, the problem would be solved we would all rest in peace.

The minute we reached Port Lincoln we two scruffy yachties made a beeline for the rat trap aisle in the supermarket. It was amusing to watch the other shoppers in the checkout line make as much space as possible between themselves and the two scruffs clutching just two traps. I declared I probably wouldn't be releasing Sir Isaac from his trap and we would need the second one to put in the ship's stores as a contingency against future acts of piracy by four legged creatures.

Within one minute of lights out Sir Isaac appeared for dinner in his usual spot. This time it was presented on a trendy wooden board. There was a bang and a squeal. My first look at him showed me I had named him correctly. He was indeed a handsome English gentleman.

Pity he decided to colonise my boat rather than stick with his loved ones onshore.

Bio: Cherylle Stone hails from Port Stephens and has sailed Australian and South West Pacific waters in a variety of craft for 45 years.

Pet Kneaded on Board
by Rachael Evans

People both on land and at sea are passionate about having their pets alongside them. We are no exception to this fine tradition.

As a family we had many discussions about what pet we could have aboard when we moved onto our yacht. We were leaving a big garden with lots of space which had been a great place for many kinds of animals over the years. But who to take with us on a 30-foot boat?

Our first choice was a dog. We have met many dogs on boats and they always seem great companions for their masters. There were a few considerations, including the size of the doggy. Tiny, it would have to be with a boat barely big enough for all of us, let alone a big dog. Small dogs are very portable, they can wear cute little life jackets and are generally non-threatening to other folks. They are also loving and would snuggle up with the kids on stormy nights. Unfortunately, we were forced to look at the flip side. We were planning coastal cruising in NZ and that comes with some distinctive issues. Having a dog would severely cramp our style and restrict the places and islands we could visit. The majority of the islands and mainland public beaches around the Hauraki Gulf, right up as far as Northland, don't allow dogs ashore. It seemed cruel to take an animal who loves to run around on the land, then not allow it to do that. We also didn't want to be the people who broke the rules on account of a desperate pooch wanting time ashore.

What about a cute moggie then? My cat, Pretzel, had been a faithful companion for 21 years. A cat would mean that we could relax about any unwanted stowaways (rats or mice). We'd already experienced the terror of a rat coming aboard. The weather had been terrible, and we'd lost our anchor and chain in a rather nasty storm. Thankfully some kind folk helped us out by allowing us to tie up to their private jetty and forage their workshop to make a grapple and retrieve the anchor. Bliss and relief! Until the next day when we saw the small rubbish bag that we'd left outside under the canopy, ripped up with the contents spilling out over the deck. In a panic we hoisted the sails and searched everywhere to find if it was still aboard, there was no sign of it then and no fresh droppings the next day. Much to our relief we were not leaving with a rat stowaway. Had we a cat we wouldn't have had that worry at all. Cats are also easy to keep and like to use a regular kitty litter space, which is pretty helpful.

Our minds were changed after we met a ranger on an island, who told us of the many times he had been contacted by people on boats, desperate to be reunited with their darling puss who "would never hurt a fly" and had somehow disappeared off their boat. Loving owners would expectantly ask if he could please contact them if puss was found. What he felt like doing was carrying a photo gallery of dead cat ID mugshots to pull out and show them, instead he contented himself with saying he was happy to call them when he found the cat dead. In one small area alone, he was trapping 11 cats a month, likely the ones being asked after, or their progeny. To him the pressure that feral cats was putting on the ecosystem was unacceptably high and often overlooked by the general public. So, it was back to the drawing board for us.

Perhaps our cockatiel Lemi could come along? Then we could be true seafaring pirates and train him to say, "Pieces of eight'. How fun would that be! We would have to clip his wings, so he too couldn't make a dash either for shore like those pesky pussies, or even worse, out to sea. We did believe that our Lemi would love life on the ocean, as he was a rescue bird cared for by a woman rehabilitating sea birds. Every time he heard a sea bird he would nut off and call very loudly to them, desperate to get their attention. This was bearable in a house, but could we stand it in a small space? And what about all the calling cards everywhere. He really wasn't poop trained and a very small cage would surely be uncomfortable. Lemi had also just befriended another cockatiel and we thought it would be sad to part the pair, breaking the newly formed bonds of bromance. That meant birds were off the menu too then.

It took a long time and much negotiation, but eventually we made a decision.

We took the plunge and our new pet was onboard after only a three day wait! We made a brilliant choice, and Sammy is our perfect companion. She's super easy to look after and thankfully doesn't shed fur, which is a huge bonus when you have two girls aboard magically losing tons of long hair every day. She only needs to be fed two tablespoons of rye every other day and offered a small drink of water to make her bubble enthusiastically when she sees me. The best bit about our beautiful pet is how amazing she smells when she's been mixed with flour and baked slowly in the galley oven for an hour. Ahh, sourdough Sammy. You, my love, are our perfect pet. You never make a fuss and you please all of the foodies in the family with the joyous loaves, buns, pizzas, pitas, and sweet scrolls that we make from you. You make our tummies content with your lactic acids, and our mouths water for your baked goodness. We cannot praise you enough.

If you too have been on the hunt for a special friend and companion to join you voyaging, you cannot possibly go past making and taking a sourdough starter 'pet'. Of all the pets imaginable, this one will readily sustain global travel and live peaceably in confined spaces wherever you go. You can even share the love by giving her babies to your friends.

So, we leave you, a happy family with a happy pet. Bon appetite and bon voyage!

Facebook: svena.sailing
Website: www.storieswithoutwords.nz

Sourdough (Rachael Evans)

Captain Patch, a Voyaging Guinea Pig
by Megan Wright

Guinea pigs are great pets for short coastal voyages. They are small, lightweight, and easy to care for. Captain Patch and his crew mates, Twilight and Drewey, regularly accompany me on short sailing trips on my parents' boat.

Guinea pigs don't need a lot of exercise and can be happy mooching around the cockpit floor when the boat is stationary. You can take them on the deck in a little harness but don't expect them to walk nicely like a dog! When underway or at night they are happy in a large cat or dog travel cage. Use wood shavings, kitty litter, or any sort of small animal bedding. Be careful that loose shavings don't get into your boat's bilge.

In addition to their own food supplies guinea pigs make short work of any salad vegetable peelings and scraps from the galley – cucumber peelings are a favourite with mine. Mix chaff and small animal pellets to keep in an airtight container on board. Carrots keep well and are good for their teeth. Celery and parsley are good dipped in water and fed on a hot day.

Captain Patch and his crew mates sit contentedly in the cockpit next to the human crew during sundowners and can be found below deck munching on their favourite foods at most other times. One of Drewey's special places was in the lockers under the cockpit combing where he would explore and sit with his nose peeking out.

There are things you need to consider before taking your guinea pig out on the water.

Guinea pigs have a low tolerance for heat. They struggle in temperatures above 30 degrees. This can be challenging in warm climates or summer on boats. There are some easy methods to help keep them cool. Keep a small spray bottle onboard and squirt a fine mist of water over them at times. If you are lucky enough to have a freezer on board you can place frozen water bottles close to the piggies. Place them near a fan or under an open hatch with a wind scoop. Keep them out of the sun though, this can be challenging when at anchor as the boat swings. Make sure they have an ample supply of fresh cool water to drink.

When underway keep the pigs secure. This can mean placing their travel boxes behind lee cloths or on the floor of a small cabin, so they don't take a tumble when the boat heels or is hit by waves or wash.

If considering taking guinea pigs onboard make sure they are used to being handled, this reduces any stress on them, and scratches on you. They are better kept in pairs (ie two males or two females) for company. Make sure they get on well together at home first.

Guinea pigs are fun to have around and despite being small they have big personalities!

Bio: Megan Wright has a TAFE Cert II in Animal Studies and Cert III in Companion Animal Services. She is a volunteer assistant animal attendant at the RSPCA and is currently training to be a zookeeper. Meg sails on her parents' Endurance 35 when not working (playing!) with all creatures great and small.

Pet Bio: Captain Patch (aka Gilfy) is a six-year-old tri-coloured, crested guinea pig who has lived with Meg since he was six weeks old. Twilight is a vocal (especially when he hears the fridge door open) six-year-old cream and white guinea pig. Drewey was a cheeky brown and ginger rescue guinea pig, with a huge personality, sadly no longer part of the crew.

Captain Patch at the helm

Drewey and his favourite locker (Meg Wright)

The Life of Pi-Rat
by Sydney Steenland (age 13)

This was my moment to work my 'pretty good' persuading skills to get what I have wanted for months. A pet. But not just any pet. In the immensely hot and humid city of Darwin (where we lived on our boat for nearly a year), my mum, brother (Indi), and I were walking to the library. My mum had just randomly said, "I want a pet rat," and that planted the 'rat for a pet' idea.

When we finally made it into our freezing library haven, I obsessively scouted for books about rats. Later that afternoon was my time to shine. I presented to Mum and Dad my pros and cons list about having a rat for a pet. I may have manipulated the data a little as the pros conveniently outweighed the cons by a landslide.

The next day we climbed into our hire car and drove to the pet store. As soon as I saw my rat I knew he was the one, mostly because he was the only rat left. But still. He was a male, black-hooded white rat that was eight weeks old. When we bought him his cage cost $64, the vet bill for neuter was $100, and he cost only $8. I had to pay back the money from the money my brother and I made from can recycle collecting. I was in love with him, I named him Jasper after this adorable baby I was babysitting, but that name did not last long. Mum came up with his most used names: 'Ratty' and 'Pirat'. Dad called him 'Feral' which he would say in a French accent, 'Fe-ral'.

While moored in the Darwin marina, Indi and I taught Ratty to run down the jetty arm, find our boat, run down the finger, jump onto the step and onto the boat. At least I think we did... the concrete jetty was hot, so that could be a big part of it. Also, maybe the fear of 'death from above' as there were eagles around. I tried to put a leash on him, but his squirmy-ness got him free from a lot of things. But sometimes he could travel in my pocket.

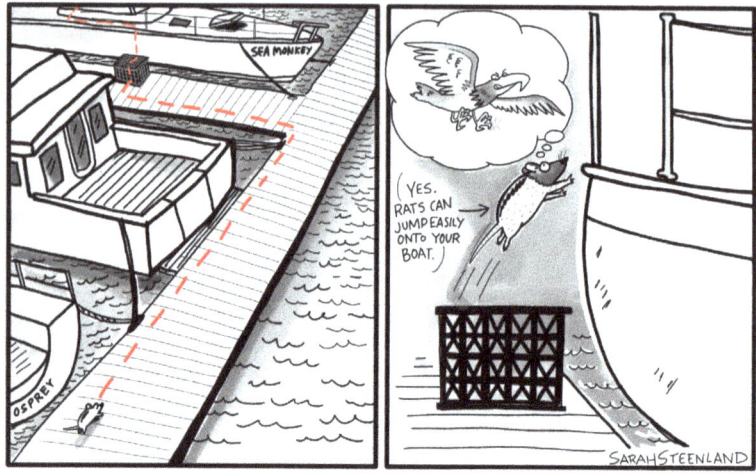

I will never forget the day we got rid of our old inflatable dingy. Mum and Dad were wheeling it on a trolley along a path to the yacht club yard with Indi and I trailing behind. I had Ratty in the 'rat-carrier' (like a briefcase to carry small pets). I thought Ratty would like a view, so I opened the case, and left it open thinking he would just sit there. I was so wrong. Ratty made a leap of faith onto the path and scurried into the nearest backyard. We knew that yard had two angry dogs that barked every time we walked to the bus stop. Indi and I freaked out and a team search started.

Mum and Dad dropped the dingy and hopped/ climbed over the fence of the yard. Mum was after Dad, she did not quite make it over the fence. Mum's shorts snagged on one of the palings. Her arms flailing all over the place, "Help! Help!". Dad turned around and lifted Mum off the fence. Indi and I guarded the outside shrubs with Dad holding the dogs off while Mum searched the yard for Ratty. Dad then joined the search. After about two minutes Dad found Ratty trying to be as flat as possible between two small palm tree stems. Terrified. He scooped him up and gave him back to me to put into the rat-carrier. I never left it open again.

A couple months later it was time to leave Australia and sail to Indonesia with the Sail Indonesia Rally. It took three days and three nights to get to Kupang, Indonesia. Customs came onto our boat, Ratty had a medical travelling certificate from the vet, but just in case, we hid him in his cage under the companionway stairs with a towel over it. The customs came inside, checked it all out and didn't see him. I think it looked very suspicious, but they didn't ask about it. Mum was sweating with anxiety. The customs man came into the aft cabin and asked mum if we had any fire arms, vaguely as he was looking at his phone. I thoughtlessly said, "Well, we have fireworks!" Mum glared at me and quietly mumbled something to me. The customs man did not hear me and asked us, "Can I have a selfie?" Mum quickly and eagerly accepted the diversion.

In Indonesia, you are treated like a celebrity because of your white skin and blond hair. Indi and I ticked all the boxes: young, cute, blond curly hair, white skin. With our best friends (the Conrad's) we had countless selfies and heaps of attention, we all decided that it would be tough being a real celebrity.

You'd think it would be quite odd for a boat pet to be scared of water. Well, Ratty had a very high level of fear of water. Think of an indoor cat, Ratty was an indoor rat. He would go stiff and dig his claws into your skin when he was outside around water. Once Mum, Indi, and I took Ratty into the shower with us and put him on the floor. He was so scared he tried to climb up our legs (this was before we knew of his fear of water, there were red marks up our legs after). Bathing Ratty was always a challenge, getting him into the bath, keeping him there, trying to scrub him without him clawing your hand. When we took him out of his bath the water would have at least five poos from Ratty being terrified.

Just before Bali, is an Island called Lombok. We would go ashore to the small bay and eat at a small yachties restaurant. A woman in her sea kayak paddled into the bay to the beach, this woman was Sandy Robson, she was paddling from Germany to Australia (it took her five years and she finished a year ago). Ratty met Sandy and she absolutely loved him. When Sandy finished her expedition, she had mentioned our family and how we had a pet rat aboard, in one of her presentations.

When anchored at Bali, the crew from *Conrad* and the *Sea Monkeys* did a road trip to visit 'Green School', Ratty included. He travelled in the rat-carrier, he got to tour Green School and we also snuck him into the bungalows. We let him run around the floor of our room. And when someone asked or guessed what was inside the rat-carrier, Ratty was either a "Sugar Glider" or a "Guinea pig".

After the road trip, our grandmother, Mazzie, came onto our boat for two weeks. For some odd reason Ratty reined his feral terror upon her. Each time she tried to pet him, Mazzie would get bitten. Ratty would stalk her, wait for her to come out of toilet, and even leap from the radio to try to attack her. Once Ratty missed his target and ended up falling into the open fridge!

With Mazzie around, every evening was drink time. Mum and Mazzie drank wine, rum, and scotch. All three of which, Ratty loved. If you were not careful, Ratty would take the opportunity to steal some alcoholic beverage – his paws gripping the rim of the cup, his neck stretched out as he gulped it down.

SARAH STEENLAND

We had a small rat cage for him, but we would get him out to play with him and for exercise. He would disappear sometimes, mostly to the sail locker where it was cool and dark. He would get inside by climbing through 'the rat highway' a space above the shelves where the cables ran through the boat. Ratty did chew the wires – Dad wasn't impressed so he made me learn how to rewire cables (he was good for our education!). When he was hiding in the sail locker, we would joke that he was secretly building a robot in there to take over the world.

Ratty ended up costing us a fair bit of money from his chewing ways. When we had the boat hauled out to get a new engine, we stayed at an apartment for a few months in Penang, Malaysia. Once he was let out of his cage, he got his 'chew on' and when we weren't looking, he had chewed two holes in the bottom of the lounge room curtain. Mum took the curtain to a local curtain maker and luckily, they had the same fabric. We replaced the left side of the curtain set. But when the curtains were closed – they were a slightly different shade to the right side! When we moved out, we left the curtains wide open and prayed the landlord didn't notice.

Sometimes we couldn't find him anywhere. We searched around the boat for so long, Mum thought he had fallen overboard, but he was just sleeping on Indi's shelf behind some books. Mum went to the toilet once, to find Ratty crawling out of a hole behind the toilet, covered in cobwebs with a few small black smudges. "What the?" exclaimed

Mum. She brought him out and I sniffed him to find that he smelled of the bilge. Hmmmmmm filthy bilge rat!

Sadly, the book I read at the library in Darwin said rats live for five years, but other research on the Internet said three years, and that was correct.

Getting older, Ratty's back legs started to give out, we had to make a ramp for him to crawl up to his hideout shelf. He was a fat rat in younger years, but he became skinny. During that time Dad, Indi, and I were in Australia. Mum had to take Ratty to the vet and put him to sleep last year.

Pi-Rat and Sydney (Sarah Steenland)

ACKNOWLEDGEMENTS

We would like to thank all the wonderful and talented authors who contributed to this anthology. Your passion and love for your pets is overwhelming. You've helped create an extraordinary book that not only is a great read, but a practical guide to help others. Most importantly, by opening your lives and sharing your stories, you've made many people laugh, and also know they are not alone in their sadness when things don't go quite as planned.

We'd also like to thank the brilliant and keen-eyed beta-readers who assisted in polishing the final draft. We are indebted to your care in helping us produce a professional publication.

Reviews
Please help more readers find Voyaging Pets by leaving a brief review on the website where you purchased this book. Many thanks.

SisterShip Magazine

SisterShip Magazine is under the SisterShip Press Pty Ltd umbrella. We publish the first global magazine written by women for women on the water.

Our bi-monthly, digital publication can be viewed here: https://issuu.com/sistershipmagazine

SisterShip Magazine's ethos:

Belong: Share passions with like-minded people;

Encourage: Support women, assist, advise, share, trust;

Inspire: Creating ideas, thoughts, hopes, dreams;

Inform: Promote safety, topical, newsy, fresh, detail; and

Entertain: Be exciting, new, fun, rich, safe, honest, reliable.

We'd love you to join us on our journey.

Best wishes,

Shelley and Jackie

www.sistershipmagazine.com

www.sistershippress.com

Contact: editor@sistershipmagazine.com

Twitter: @SisterShipMag

Instagram: @sistershipmagazine

Facebook: SisterShip Magazine, SisterShip Press, SisterShip Book Club

www.ingramcontent.com/pod-product-compliance
Lightning Source LLC
Chambersburg PA
CBHW040551010526
44110CB00054B/2640